Bill Muehl

IN REFLECTION

Bill Muehl
IN REFLECTION

Opinion Columns Over Three Decades

E. William Muehl

edited by Jon F. McKenna
with a foreword by Harry B. Adams

Yale University Divinity School
New Haven, Connecticut

Contents

Foreword

For over twenty years, Bill Muehl wrote his column of opinion for *Reflection*, a journal of the Yale Divinity School. During all of those years I served as the editor of the journal, and was always convinced that most readers of the magazine turned first to read what Bill had to say. Although there was no comprehensive survey to confirm my conviction, I talked to enough people to know that Bill's column was provocative and stimulating, and that it was, in fact, the first thing read.

With pointed wit and penetrating insight, Bill Muehl addressed himself to issues of the church and of the world. He had a remarkable capacity to take some ordinary event and use it to help readers see the folly of the world or the wisdom of the Gospel in fresh perspective. At times he stirred vigorous responses from people who disagreed with him, which gave testimony that he was dealing with significant issues and speaking with uncommon clarity.

It is a delight indeed to have these articles, selected and sometimes revised by Bill, brought together in this little book. I am confident that they will be read again and again with pleasure and with profit.

Thanks go to Jon McKenna and Barbara Blodgett at the Divinity School for editorial work, to Yale University Printing Service for graphic design, and to Lithoprint, Inc. of North Haven for composing and printing this volume.

Harry B. Adams
Chaplain, Yale University
and Master of Trumbull College

To Hell with Acceptance!
March, 1967

If by the time this bit of wisdom reaches its intended public I have been separated from the faculty of the Divinity School, let none be greatly surprised. The reason for my dismissal will not be the manifest incompetence which I have become so adept at concealing over the years. But disorderly conduct in Chapel. Because the next time someone stands up in the pulpit and tells me that I am "accepted" and implies that I should be greatly comforted by that announcement, I am going to rise and make quite specific suggestions about the appropriate disposition of that helpful word!

Years ago we were told that God *loves* us. And during the period in which logistical problems made it necessary for me to attend a Southern Presbyterian Church I even learned several songs committed to that proposition. We used to sing them in Sunday School, whenever we could get the teacher to stop talking about our unclean thoughts long enough to strike a chord on the piano.

But as I was saying before Calvin broke in, the proclamation that one has been "accepted" by God is one of the worst bits of bad news ever to issue from the murky caverns of Teutonic theology. Who wants to be accepted? I certainly don't. And neither, I suspect, does the rest of the human race which has not been infected by ordination. We want to be *loved.* And there is a terrible chasm fixed between love and acceptance.

To be loved gives human beings a sense of personal significance. Because in spite of all the nonsense spoken by theologians and psychotherapists, love is both demanding and judging. It attaches itself to the particular and peculiar qualities of the beloved. It delights in his or her virtues and victories and is saddened by his or her vices and defeats. And in time it can be destroyed by the radical deterioration of the beloved's personality. My wife loves me, William Muehl, an aging, paunchy, bad-tempered individual with many high hopes and a few modest achievements to his credit. She does not love an abstraction, a sub-unit in some homogenized human mass. And I feel the same way about her. (Not that *she* is paunchy and bad tempered, for pity's sake!)

In the days when the human problem was an over-developed, highly legalistic sense of the meaning of every action, when humanity was plagued by the conviction that each deed had a measurable quantity of power to save or damn, the suggestion that God's ego is not all *that* involved in the details of the human enterprise was undoubtedly reassuring. (If I had been able to dredge up any really unclean thoughts back there in Louisville at the age of seven, it might have comforted me to believe that I could enjoy one from time to time without fear of being ignited by some cosmic pyromaniac!)

The problem facing us today, however, is not an excess of meaning in history but the suspicion that history is wholly *without* meaning. We no longer find people huddled around ancient altars trying fearfully to work out the complex implications of divine commandments. On the contrary, we see them wandering about at loose ends persuaded that no one gives a damn about what happens anywhere in the cosmos. To tell such aimless creatures that God does not keep score is hardly good news. It is actually the worst possible news that anyone could proclaim.

A God who loves men and women, specific men and women, with a love which reflects and responds to variable qualities in each one of them gives dignity to life and meaning to history. But a God who "accepts" us without regard to those attributes which distinguish one character and caliber from another destroys the whole concept of human personality.

So, Brothers and Sisters, be of good cheer. You are *not* accepted. You are loved. And what is equally important, you still have the freedom to reject that love and go to Hell!

This column brought a note from a Harvard Divinity student thanking me for having "demolished Professor Tillich!" I just don't know my own strength.

A Quaint Liturgical Proposal

March, 1968

In spite of the current revival of interest in Christian liturgy among Protestants and the radical nature of much that is being done in avant-garde worship services, there has been no serious proposal that the Crucifix be restored to some central place in the life of the churches. And yet if I were asked to name the religious symbol which has potentially the greatest meaning for people today, it would be the image of Christ *on the Cross.*

One need not accept the most extravagant romanticism about the "Christ figure" in recent fiction to understand that the concept of the suffering God has great meaning for men and women in our time. Many people who are untouched by every other form of Christian affirmation are deeply moved by the vision of the God-Man who is betrayed, seized, mocked, tortured and killed — far more deeply moved than they ever can be by the mythology of the Resurrection and the symbolism of the empty tomb.

The day when people were content to define salvation as some kind of escape from "this world" has happily long since gone. The advance of human knowledge has at many points failed dismally to fulfill its own bright promises. Humanity neither understands the mystery of being nor controls its own destiny. But it *has* become able to see its existence as an integral part of the world in which it is lived. Human beings no longer feel compelled or willing to state their significance in terms of absolute differences be-

4

tween themselves and the so-called "natural order." Life can be and often is "mean, nasty, brutish and short." But this world is humanity's home, the milieu in which the love of God makes possible all the fulfillment that any finite being can expect. We are not *of* the world originally. But thanks to the redemptive surrender of God in Christ we have become the world's ultimate dimension. We have been given the power not to transcend history but to transform it. Whatever eternal life may have meant to our grandparents, it is for most of us life raised to the nth degree, not a refined and dehydrated spirituality.

The inadequacy of the barren Cross that stands upon Protestant altars is that, whatever its primitive significance, it now bespeaks a meaning *imposed retroactively* upon life. It seems to suggest that God's coming into history was really just a prelude to the Great Escape on Easter morning, that the value of history is determined by the a-historical, by what happens above and beyond it.

Let's put the problem another way: I strongly suspect that for most of us Easter is *the* ultimate anti-climax. The high point of Holy Week is Good Friday. Not the Empty Tomb but the Crucifixion. Because, you see, what human beings need desperately to believe is that what happens *here and now,* what they endure in every moment of time, has an inherent meaning that is given by the grace of God. But by the grace of God's entrance and involvement, not God's miraculous escape. It is not Easter which redeems the horror of Good Friday. It is, rather, Good Friday which bestows meaning upon the pallid mystery of Easter. Men and women do not bear with faithful patience the bloody tragedy of Calvary because they know that it will be made abundant joy two days later. They bear with considerable *im*patience the improbabilities of Easter because of what happened on the Cross.

Why then are we so fearful of the Crucifix? Precisely because of its true centrality in the life of faith. Because it binds us and our hopes so strongly to the God who is *in* history. Because it assails the sentimental assurance that God stands waiting to greet and vindicate us just beyond the long shadows of our mortal Lent. Because it implies so strongly that the real power of redeeming love is in the living, suffering and dying, not in the rising again. Thus, it puts upon our hearts and consciences burdens far heavier than that mobile boulder which figures so prominently in the Great Escape.

A lot of nonsense has been uttered under the heading "the Death of God." But perhaps something of the response that the phrase has elicited from many thoughtful people can be understood in terms of what I have been saying. Better a God who dies and who in dying gives eternal meaning to history than a God whose Resurrection impugns the significance of existence itself.

One of my favorite former students complained that this sounded too much like "the young Karl Barth." Boy, these kids know how to hurt!

That Damned Word

January, 1969

Some years ago, when Yale University was struggling to keep me from being lured away by one of the many centers of higher learning which are constantly vying for my services, the faculty at the Divinity School decided to promote me to what Hal Luccock insisted upon calling "a fool professor." Believe it or not, this move involved some tricky maneuvering in the area of nomenclature. I had begun my career teaching public speaking. But since my interests had risen above the diaphragm, that designation seemed somehow inadequate. At one point the title "Christian Communication" was proposed . . . and Whitney Griswold went up the wall. ("Let Marburg or Gottingen have him rather than put that damned word in our faculty roster!") So I became Professor of Practical Theology, which is a great conversation piece.

President Griswold's reaction to the word "communication" is not an uncommon one. It is often assumed, especially in academic circles, that "communication" consists of vulgarizing or at least over-simplifying something in order to make it available to the common ear. And fairness compels me to admit that this assumption is not wholly unfounded. There *are* those whose principle of communication is to make the complex simple and turn all poetry into prose.

It seems to me increasingly important, however, to point out, especially to the church, that this is not necessarily the basis of communication. The effort to talk about the Christian gospel in understandable ways need not mean the reduction of its mysteries to monosyllabic declarative sentences. It *can* mean and *should* mean the insistence that human beings see their own lives and the history of which they are parts as infinitely complex, composed of awful depths and majestic heights.

The average churchgoer takes into the pew on Sunday what might be called a three-dimensional view of human existence. He or she tends to believe that all truly important matters are essentially simple and can be dealt with adequately in terms of the canons of common sense. In more paranoid moments he or she suspects that profundity is an intellectual plot against the natural law. In more tolerant moods it is recognized as the eccentric passion of harmless cranks.

One of the most dangerous mistakes that any Christian preacher or teacher can make is to accept, even for the purposes of evangelism, this radical oversimplification of the truth. The moment people try to relate a four-dimensional gospel to a three-dimensional view of reality they find themselves with one dimension left over. This rhetorical remainder is usually defined as "theology," something irrelevant to the real world, which courteous people tolerate as a concession to the clergy. There are few things more frustrating than the effort to preach the gospel persuasively under such conditions. Eventually the victim of this fatal disjunction either abandons the gospel and settles for high-minded discourses on prudential wisdom or denounces "relevance" as a dirty word and delivers lectures, loaded with theological integrity, to which no one listens.

Obviously effective communication begins by inviting or compelling the listener to think in terms of the real world and recognize its fearful complexity. For it is only as one is willing to do this that he or she will become able to identify the questions with which Christian faith is concerned and admit the responsibility of the church to address those questions intelligently.

But here we face a substantial theological problem, do we not? A great deal of traditional Christian theology lacks what might be called a doctrine of the mind. That is to say, millions of men and women grow up in the church without ever hearing it suggested that there may be an intellectual component to salvation. Year after year they receive the promise that faith is the gift of grace wholly unrelated to the uses of intelligence. So they come in time to believe that, whatever its value in the more practical affairs of life, thought has no significant function in the realm of piety. And God help the preacher who suggests otherwise!

It seems quite clear to me, however, that there can be no effective proclamation of the gospel in our sophisticated age without a radical revision of the popular view of the human being's intellectual responsibilities. Or to put it in other words, the problem of communication in the church today is basically a vexatious *theological* problem. No wonder so many of our theologians share Whitney Griswold's disdain for "that damned word."

I am not sure whether to feel flattered or insulted that the faculty has decided to "beef up" the Divinity School's offerings in the field on my retirement.

The Baptism of Spittle

January, 1970

In the movie version of Shaw's *Major Barbara* there is a particular scene which has always seemed to me worth the price of admission in itself. It occurs during a street corner evangelistic meeting conducted by the Salvation Army. Major Barbara and her cohorts have made their way to the heart of the London slums with fanfare and tattoo. Here, fearful but resolute, they form a circle and begin to give testimony.

The high point in their performance comes when a former boxer, a man who claims to have been saved from the prize ring by an act of Providence, steps forward to offer his witness. He is large, well-muscled, and his face bears the evidence of his former profession. So thoroughly scarred is his countenance that one need not be a cynic to suspect that the Holy Spirit was only one step ahead of the Royal Boxing Commission in putting an end to his career.

As the ex-pug speaks his too familiar piece the crowd gets somewhat out of hand. And one young tough elbows the others aside, leans forward and spits into the old battler's face.

For a long moment the Holy Spirit seems about to lose out to something more human. The boxer's eyes flash. His biceps strain. His heavy hands knot into threatening clubs. And the man who did the spitting, aware that he has taken on more than he can handle, draws nervously back into the crowd.

But suddenly a change comes over the insulted speaker. His

taut look eases. His teeth unclench. The raised fists fall back to his sides. And with a look of beatific joy on his features, he lifts his spit-stained face to the heavens and cries, "Ah, the glory of it! The glory of it! That I should be found worthy to be spat upon for the gospel!"

There is, it would seem, something appealing to being "spat upon for the gospel." As unpopular as other kinds of martyrdom may be, this particular form appears to have a perverse attractiveness to it. For, you see, when one tries to claim kinship with Christ on the basis of one's piety, dedication or sacrificial love, the absurdity of the pretension becomes immediately obvious. The immensity of the presumption is its own refutation.

But suppose I claim kinship with Christ on the basis of rejection. The measure of the validity of this claim is now not my own stature but the violence of others. They hated him, and they hate *me*. They spat upon him, and they spit upon *me*. Even his friends turned away, and so do *mine*.

This device makes Christ my own at cut-rate prices. It gives dignity to my social disasters, excuses my poor manners, redeems me from having to confront all that is crude, unlovely and graceless in myself. The principle at work here is one with which we are familiar: If spitting is unavoidable, testify and enjoy it.

The more traditional manifestations of this mood are easily indicated, and few will rise to their defense. There are evangelists, for example, who are clearly more eager to be rejected than they are to be heard. And the variety of them is great. It runs from the street corner trumpeter whose message is as out of tune as his music, to the divinity student preacher who is determined to protect the offensiveness of the gospel by proclaiming it in polysyllabic obscurities. What all these have in common is a kind of joy in being failures for Christ and thus grasping at subtle equality with him whom they cannot hope to equal in godliness.

Today this once furtive and often unrecognized device has come above ground and taken on the dimensions of a mass movement. One suspects that significant segments of the clergy are trying to conceal from themselves and the world at large the *real* scandal of the cross by modes of speech, dress and general deportment which are offensive inherently rather than incidentally.

"Let no one willfully misunderstand me." I am not referring here to the authentic radical, the person who puts life and career on the line. Nor would I indict those for whom the smashing of convention is merely the means of uncovering what is true. I have in mind, rather, those who practice the forms of the prophetic without its substance, who ape the symbolic style of radical commitment while carefully exercising a worldly prudence, who adopt as mere personal eccentricities the speech and demeanor which mark a genuinely innovative ministry.

It is not pleasant to be spat upon. But it is often a small price to pay for the sense of being where the action is, while abiding under the shadow of the establishment.

Since reading the spy novels of LeCarre, I have begun to suspect that the fellow who did the spitting may have been a Salvation Army "mole" who had been planted in the crowd to provoke just such an occasion for the pug's dramatic witness.

The Good Bad-Guy

March, 1970

Some years ago *The New Yorker* carried a cartoon in which two middle-aged women were shown discussing a couple that had just entered the room. "Oh, she's a perfect saint," one of them was saying, "but, of course, he's much more of a person."

This kind of distinction between saintliness on the one hand and vital humanity on the other is not unfamiliar to us. It is regularly dramatized in fiction of every sort and is one of the common sub-themes in countless movies and television shows. More often than not the case is made indirectly, and we are left to infer the brutal truth for ourselves. But the point is generally too obvious to be missed.

The most common vehicle for this "moral" is a story in which the hero is a villain who converts to righteousness at some critical juncture and, using the arts which he has acquired during his years of depravity, works prodigies of valor, while the decent citizens of the community hide behind shuttered windows until the danger has passed.

I am thinking, for example, of the professional gunfighter who turns on his own gang and foils their foul machinations because a small child has looked trustingly into his eyes. Or the dance hall girl who becomes a virtual Florence Nightingale when a mine disaster injures a large number of men, and the church ladies cannot bring themselves to look upon burly bleeding bodies in various stages of dishabille. One dramatic liturgy after another drives the point home: Good people are timid and ineffectual in a crisis. Bad people are courageous and resourceful.

The primary source of this myth is obviously human sinfulness. Evil hates good and has learned to express its resentment by the use of ridicule. That which is corrupt in each of us enjoys attributing base motives and cowardly behavior to virtue, our own and that of others. And conversely, the devil persuades us, if he can, that irresponsible self-indulgence is a great character builder. This is one theological lesson that the manipulators of the mass media have learned thoroughly.

But there is more to the paradox of the good bad-guy in fiction than can be explained by original sin. The problem is in part a reflection of the difficulty which people face when they try to define human personality in terms of Christian love. Love is by its very nature self-*giving* not self-*asserting.* It draws men and women into kinds of fellowship which not only tear down interpersonal barriers but often blur interpersonal boundaries as well. We all sense this fact of life. And we suspect that the saint must be dull, because he or she will not defend those lines by which the individual is made a unique and interesting personality.

Villains are by definition not inhibited by the canons of piety. Thus, they are free to assert themselves, i.e. discover and express their selfhood in a great variety of ways. They do a lot of damage in the process. But, so goes the myth, they also develop the virtues of strength and confidence which are rooted in a well-defined self-image. When these values are summoned forth by a crisis of some kind the bad guy is *able* to convert, because even a radical change of heart does not threaten his secure personality. And following his conversion he is left with a residue of villainous cunning to put at the disposal of some good cause.

Like most popular myths about the nature of humanity, the

good bad-guy paradox involves numerous distortions of the truth. But the eagerness with which it is received and believed by masses of people suggests that one of the major unfinished tasks of Christian theology is the formulation of an adequate doctrine of Christian self-assertion.

This was written when the summons of the gospel seemed to be to sacrificial love rather than aggressive self-fulfillment.

The Viscous Circle

May, 1970

Far be it from me to call attention to anything as obvious as the circular nature of history. Especially since that biblical favorite of mine, Koheleth, did the job so splendidly in his "wee bookie." But I do find myself both charmed and amused by the enthusiasm with which a new generation of Christians is "discovering" and adapting some of the oldest traditions of the church, traditions which its immediate predecessors in the faith cast aside with scornful impatience.

Take, for example, the practice of starting a service of worship with solemn procession, including flags, banners, cross bearers and miscellaneous ministers of various degrees of dignity. When I was a kid attending a "high" Episcopal Church this was common practice. And we acolytes used to fight for the right to swing the incense pot! (I had a tendency to chicken out when it came to the full over-hand arc, so the job seldom came my way.)

Well, I ended up in a Southern Presbyterian Church for a few years, as faithful readers of this column will recall, and was quickly weaned away from such popery. But now, behold, processions with banners, flags, etc. are once more becoming the order of the day in churches of all sorts and descriptions. Even incense has reappeared, in some cases to cover up the smell of pot.

Or consider the practice of asking for testimony and prayers from members of the congregation speaking up from their places in the pews. Only recently frowned upon as evidence of an unseemly enthusiasm, it is being gleefully embraced by the avant-garde, which is all for involvement. And we now have moments set aside between our electronic guitar selections for expressions of community and personal concerns.

Don't get me wrong. I am very much in favor of such forms of enrichment. They strike me as preferable to the morbid classicism of the early Sixties, when groups of students and more mature theologians spent hours trying to "purify" Protestant liturgies by pouring through history books seeking to discover just how Martin Luther celebrated the Holy Eucharist or whether John Calvin put the Lord's Prayer before or after the sermon.

As a matter of solemn fact I have argued for years that there is as much agape present in a well-run church supper as in the most valid Mass. The sight of some of the laity scurrying about a basement kitchen preparing fried chicken while others make small talk in the adjacent dining room is one to warm the heart. And when at last the steaming casseroles, crisp salads and proud pies have been spread out on trestled tables ready to be consumed on behalf of the Parsonage Maintenance Fund, Jesus Christ seems more visibly present than he ever is in a tray of grape juice self-consciously passed from hand to hand on Sunday morning. The words "fellowship" and "community" came to have their real meaning for me in just such settings.

Whatever one may feel about particular adaptations of older festivals, it is heartening to see young church members learning that many of the popular folk rituals of the local church served a purpose which is not fully met by either sound doctrine or social zeal. Who can tell? One of these days an imaginative person might even rediscover what we used to call the "Sunday School."

It intrigues me to notice that the avant-garde is deeply "into" the folk rituals of Latin America as expression of indigenous piety, while still disdainful of their parallels in North American churches.

Canned Goods and Kings

March, 1971

When I was a small boy I once ran a thriving grocery store under the family dinner table. Not on remnants of food dropped or thrown there during meals, although Grandpa did get a bit careless in his declining years, but with canned goods taken from the kitchen pantry. I would drape a blanket over the mahogany roof to make side walls, heap a nice variety of soups, vegetables and luncheon meats in one corner and sell these items back to my parents at amazingly low prices. One who shopped carefully might have fed a family of five for a full week on something less than a dollar.

The business was doing remarkably well until I tried to expand by inviting kids from the neighborhood to patronize it. Then my father stepped in, and I was compelled to liquidate rapidly. The building metamorphosed into a combination frontier stockade and pirate ship, to the great dismay of hostile Indians and honest seafarers.

It took a great deal of patient explaining on Dad's part, however, to make me understand the flaw in my formula for success. And when the truth finally dawned something beautiful went out of life. Reinhold Neibuhr, who was at that time pastor of a church just up the street, gained a disciple, although he lost a really good buy in Campbell's beans.

I was reminded of that experience many years later by a

drawing room comedy about the tribulations of an aristocratic English family facing social revolution. At one point in the second act the eldest son faced his father and delivered a shrill diatribe against the "establishment." He made it quite clear that he was ashamed of his antecedents, disgusted with his class and wanted nothing further to do with his old man.

"So far as I am concerned," he concluded, "you no longer exist."

Father took this with admirable Chesterfieldian calm, and when it ended, asked quietly, "That's all very well, but how do you propose to live?"

The young man threw back his shoulders, thrust out his chin defiantly and replied, "I shall simply have to learn to get by on my allowance."

These two incidents seem to me paradigmatic of one of the major frustrations of modern rebels. They are tempted to take for granted a complex of social structures and dynamisms which make up something called the "status quo" and from which they derive many of the values by which they are moved to rebellion. And to the degree that they do not recognize this paradox they formulate ideologies which are woefully out of touch with reality.

Both the New Right and the New Left, for example, are flirting with various forms of anarchy in their prescriptions for radical change. Many of their spokesmen feel passionately that our political institutions are worse than the individuals who compose them and that, left to themselves, "the people" will generate new communities of voluntary cooperation. This is an ancient and honored hope, and its contemporary champions often expound it with an earnestness born of authentic idealism.

The problem is that their doctrine of human nature is a part of our common "allowance," a legacy from centuries of relatively ordered political process. What the "establishment" has contributed to the humane impulses of civilized humanity is taken for granted, while its crimes are writ large and endlessly repeated. It is easy to forget that the ghastly tyranny of the Third Reich was built upon the doctrines of the Nazi Party, a *voluntary* association of like-minded (sic) individuals. And when one is most disturbed about the sins of big government it is important to remember what locally based White Citizens Councils have contributed to oppressive practices in our society. As the distinguished political scientist James Roche has pointed out, in recent decades the most dramatic humanizing changes in the United States have been sponsored by the Federal Government and achieved over the stubborn resistance of states and cities.

I am not suggesting that those who benefit from a political order have no right to condemn it and agitate for revolution. But it is vitally important, perhaps especially important, for radical reformers to appreciate what they owe to the past. Failing to do so, they may start out for the grocery store — and end up walking the plank!

The more cynical profess to see a conservative cloud no bigger than a human hand on the horizon in this column. Not true! The McGovern campaign which came later generated that atmospheric change.

*Response to an Art School Professor Who Claims That
Picasso's "Guernica" Communicates More Than
Photographs of the Victims of Hiroshima*

May, 1971

They say when Heinrich Himmler saw
His first mass execution of the Jews
He wept.
He rushed into the line of rifle fire,
And screamed that it must stop.
Then when it did he fell down
There on the German ground before his men
And vomited.
They had to help him back into his car,
(A big Mercedes-Benz, I think it was.)
Glasses broken, peaked cap askew;
And on the long ride into town
He cried and cried, and he
Was sick again.

Poor Heinrich, "Gentle Heinrich,"
Hitler called him, back in the Beer Hall days.
He wasn't meant to be a camera,
Catching representational views of life.
He preferred his truth in abstract form,
In charts and graphs and veiled languages.
"A final solution to the Jewish problem."

"The purification of the Nordic race."
And so he sat there at his desk
Doing his paper work,
While sealed boxcars moved into the East
And Nordic air thickened with Jewish smoke.

I saw a painting just the other day,
"Man's Cruelty to Man," the label said.
It was a splendid thing, I'm sure.
All jagged streaks, dark shadows, broken lines.
I longed to take it home with me,
To hang it on the wall,
And have my friends come in to view
This stark expression of the human scene.
Then we would stand there sipping sherry,
Nibbling bits of cheese,
And vow as how it takes an artist's touch
To capture life in depth.

If one must look on truth,
It's best done so.
No falling on the ground before the world.
No puking on the rug, no sour smells.
But just a kind of clever indoor game.
O, God, I wish man's cruelty to man
Would stay there on the wall inside its frame!

Love Boldly!

November, 1971

Years ago Morton Cronin wrote an article for *The Nation* in which he decried what he called "the tyranny of democratic manners." In modern America, he pointed out, human beings are expected to relate to one another in rituals which deny all differences of rank and power. Workers on the assembly line are not only allowed but encouraged to call the foreman by his first name. When a rising young junior executive enters the office of the firm's president he or she is expected to perch on the edge of the desk, show the latest pictures of the family and kid the boss about their last golf game. Ivy League professors disdain the use of their titles and make a great point of being called "Mister."

Now if this compulsive equalitarianism reflected accurately the facts of life in our society, Cronin concluded, it might not be disturbing. But beneath the surface of this ultra-democracy, Americans are separated by deep differences of prestige, wealth and power. When these are confronted honestly it is always possible to cope with them and minimize their negative consequences. So long as the liturgies of daily life keep us mindful of the tensions, healthy and unhealthy, in the community, we can deal with them responsibly. When, however, the superficial symbols of equality are used to *conceal* degrees of rank and authority they become the facade behind which various forms of painful insecurity flourish.

There is a soundness in this argument which Christians

should be the first to recognize. The human personality is in many respects a fragile thing, and individual uniqueness has an almost gossamer quality to it. The little gestures by which we acknowledge differences and preserve distance between individuals have more importance than the democratic ethos is inclined to recognize. What appears at first glance to be meaningless protocol or archaic courtesy may actually be essential to the preservation of cherished personal attributes. And those who are denied socially acceptable defenses may take refuge in neurotic estrangement from the press of humanity around them.

Cronin points out, for example, that Ivy League professors who make such a point of eschewing designations of rank are often less available to their students or more defensive in dealing with them than the state university teacher whose insistence upon his or her titles (I once called my host "Mister" and heard him murmur quietly, "Doctor") allows him or her to be more relaxed in substantive terms. These latter can afford to expose themselves to faculty-student contact, because they have been provided by protocol with defenses behind which they can take shelter from excessive interpersonal trespass.

I have long felt that something of this same kind of paradox vexes the course of Christian love. The kind of love to which men and women are exhorted by the New Testament takes little or no account of qualitative distinctions. It bids us love one another as Christ loves us without regard for the eccentricities which differentiate one personality from another.

But most of us recognize, do we not, that it is the eccentricities which distinguish each of us from all others. And we have the uneasy feeling that any affection which leaves them out of account is a fairly meaningless formality. So we tend to be fearful of Christian love, because we suspect that to love everyone very much is to love no one at all. And surely we have all met Christians whose behavior bears out such suspicions.

A large part of what it means to be finite is that our affections will inevitably attach themselves to *particular* rather than *universal* human attributes. When we love others for what they alone possess our love enhances their personalities. But when we love people for what they have in common with the human race in general they quite rightly fear that the relationship threatens their individuality.

It is surely not the least of the gifts of the Cross that it frees us to love as finite beings, to respond passionately to those peculiar characteristics which define other personalities, knowing that by God's grace we can be forgiven the inevitable exclusiveness of our affections.

If I have an identifiable Christology, its nascent murmurs can be heard here.

A Bumper Crop of Pietists

January, 1972

I have often wondered whatever became of the people who used to write inspirational counsels on roadside rocks and barns. You know the kind of thing I mean: "Prepare to meet thy God!" —"The wages of sin is death." — "Impeach Earl Warren!" — and other salvific sentiments. Those evangelistic efforts livened up many a dull mile of family automobile travel when I was a kid.

I used to bet my younger brother that I could spot more of them on my side of the car than he could on his. And since I always contrived to be seated on the right hand side of the car, I invariably won. He was ten years old before he discovered the secret of my success, and shortly thereafter he "accidentally" flushed my pet chameleon down the toilet.

But as I started to say, I think that I have finally learned the fate of those who provided the occasions for one of my more imaginative kinds of sin. They have taken up a new vocation and now compose bumper stickers for the vehicles whose riders they used to accost from the roadside.

Drive along any street and read as you ride the verbal expressions of a new pietism: "War is bad for children." — "Another family for peace." — "Stop all pollution." — "Guns can kill."

Now there is nothing really wrong with such vehicular adornments. Just as there was nothing wrong with writing "Jesus saves" on rock outcroppings or spiritually oriented barns. (I prefer them to their counterparts on the right: "America, love it or leave it." — "Support your local police.") But they bespeak a kind of naive faith in the power of moral exhortation. They are what would at one time have been called "pious ejaculations." And they have all the practical force of a Buddhist prayer wheel. One suspects, and I think with reason, that the people who wrote on rocks did little else to improve the lot of the human race. And I suspect that the same is true of those who proclaim their devotion to purity slightly to the northeast of their exhaust pipes.

It is not the least of the crimes of the war in Viet Nam that it has saddled a whole generation with a moralistic fervor that makes a plausible substitute for intelligence. Problems of massive complexity are being distilled by the heat of rhetoric into simple solutions. Let some well-meaning non-entity rise to demand an end to the war in Asia or to the contamination of our waterways, and before he has gotten back to his seat some other well-meaning non-entity will have risen to nominate him for the Presidency of the United States. There are cars in the parking lots at Yale bearing on their bumpers such propositions as "Wilbur B. Prone in '72." And when you ask about the identity of Mr. Prone you will be told with indignation that he is, as all right-thinking people know, the courageous Cook County Dog Warden who at a meeting of the Friends of Furbearers openly called Mayor Daley of Chicago a "fathead."

Well, the Mayor of Chicago is not one of my favorite people. But calling him a "fathead" does not qualify anyone to be anything, except a *former* employee of Cook County.

There was a time in American life when we tended to base ethical judgments on a simplistic analysis of individual character. If a person abstained from the use of spirits, taught a church Bible study class and was reasonably discreet about adultery, his opinion on many public questions was likely to be highly regarded. And if he was so minded he might easily be hailed as God's gift to political reform. More damned scoundrels rode into office on the coattails of the Anti-Saloon League than the railroads could afford to buy. And one of the foulest racists in the United States Senate some years ago was regularly supported for re-election by religious leaders, because he taught the largest Sunday School class in the state.

We laugh or sneer at such naivete these days. But I have an uneasy feeling that a great many Americans are guilty of the same kinds of feelings about social issues in our own time. And we are as tempted as our grandparents to define heroism in painfully simplistic terms. If a person takes a dramatic stand on one or two critical issues such as peace and ecological sanity, we tend to invest him with the qualities of greatness asking little about the details of his program or the political realism of our support. We encourage politicians to become single-issue in their public postures, and more and more one-sided in their rhetoric. Until at last they have alienated all but the pure in heart and have doomed our cause to inevitable defeat.

The desire to make ethical decisions the occasions for public displays of personal purity is not limited to traditional pietists. It is as common among pacifists as among teetotalers. And its outward and visible signs are as obvious on bumpers as on barns.

Both the Pro-lifers and the Pro-choicers could take a bit of useful coaching from this one.

Live a Little

May, 1972

During my early days on the New Haven Board of Aldermen I had occasion to argue with one of my black colleagues about his responsibility to the ghetto which had elected him. By and large he had a solid record on social legislation. But on a particular issue he seemed to me more concerned with his own political future than with the welfare of his constituents. And I was determined to save his soul.

My friend listened patiently for a time and then with a tired smile interrupted me. "You know, Muehl, there is a very important thing that you had better learn about black people in this country. We're willing to make sacrifices to improve things for one another. But we don't want to spend all of our lives *improving* our lives. We want to spend some of our lives just *living*."

I was too passionately involved then in a particular problem to appreciate the wisdom of that comment. But with the passage of time I have come to see that it applies not simply to black people but to all people. In even the most cruelly deprived circumstances there are joys and satisfactions to be found. And we want at least a chance to sample some of them.

It was one of the weaknesses of the social gospel that it often seemed to ignore this basic fact and let itself become a summons to perpetual self-sacrifice. Many dedicated men and women tired of being marshalled behind some new banner every Sunday morning and made to feel callous if they were able to enjoy their lives even in the face of injustice.

I suspect that the zeal of the contemporary church for a theology of "celebration" reflects a reaction against such dour discipleship, as does the return to privatistic mysticism by many younger Christians. No one wants to spend his or her whole life on the barricades. And we reject a religion which asks us to do so.

Now note how craftily I have sneaked up on women! For what I am saying does have special relevance for their struggle for liberation.

No one of sound mind denies the right of women to greater dignity, freedom and opportunity than they have had in the past. From subtle cultural factors to explicit legal discrimination the spectrum of their oppression is a broad one. A great deal is needed in the field of legislation in order to raze the barriers which deny women full human equality. And even more will have to be done to dissipate the atmospheric conditions which induce feelings of inferiority.

It would be unfortunate, however, if any considerable number of women set out to make their crusade a full time occupation and began to measure their own or their sisters' worth only by the number of hours spent on the barricades. For in spite of the obvious need for institutional changes in the process of liberation such reforms will be futile if they thicken the atmosphere of internecine aggressiveness in which we all suffer.

We know from sad experience that nations in conflict often take on the worst features of their enemies and lose the values for which they fight. Wars for democracy have a tendency to create everything but democracy.

The traditional relationship between the sexes has undercut the freedom of women at far too many points. But in the paradoxical manner of things in a fallen creation it has also engendered some of the richest sensitivities in our culture. And a full-time barricade psychology could irreparably damage the human dignity which women seek to enhance.

Don't ever try to spit into a tornado!

The Grace of Hypocrisy

November, 1972

One of the most controversial characters in the Bible is the tax collector who is used by Jesus in the 18th chapter of Luke to rebuke the self-righteousness of the Pharisees. Preachers love him. Most laymen hate his humble guts.

The antagonism between the two points of view is both deep and instructive. Its chief cause is, I suppose, the problem of grace. Clergy are hung up on divine grace and haunted by the specter of works righteousness. The laity, on the other hand, give a high priority to seeing that the celestial welfare rolls are not overloaded with deadbeats. (In a memorable cartoon some years ago Peter is shown complaining to Christ: "How can I implement intelligent policy at the gates when your mother keeps letting people in the back door?")

But there is another aspect to this controversy about the tax collector, one which runs to the psychological rather than the theological implications of the story.

Preachers are understandably hard on hypocrites. They have not only scriptural authority but a good deal of pastoral experience to fire up their zeal on the subject. The human habit of talking one way and acting another can make the task of ministry both difficult and discouraging. And it gives enemies of the faith a debating point which not even German theology can explain away! Small wonder that hypocrisy engenders some of the pulpit's most prophetic utterances.

The laity, however, tend to see the gap between word and deed in a somewhat different light. For many of them it symbolizes a salutary consciousness of the difference between right and wrong. People who feel guilty enough about their behavior to lie, they argue, have taken one very long step toward amendment of life. And they have given their consciences a good deal of leverage to use in lifting the standard of their future conduct. When men and women say one thing and do another they inevitably come under the judgment of consistency.

I remember an occasion during the last days of World War II ("The big one!") when an informal group of faculty members at the Divinity School got into a discussion of the relative dangers posed by Fascism and Communism as anti-Christian ideologies. Some argued that Fascism was the less formidable enemy because of its open hostility to the Christian view of human nature and history. No one could ever be deceived about its intentions, they contended. Communism, rather, is the more subtle foe. It disguises its materialistic philosophy in democratic and humanitarian language which can mislead the unwary.

Without denying the facts underlying this position I sided with those who feared Fascism more deeply. Communism's verbal commitments to human community, peace and justice, I insisted, gives its victims some basis on which to seek redress. The very fact that Communist leaders have to lie to their own people about the implications of their doctrine somewhat inhibits the directness and efficiency with which they can operate. Fascists, on the other hand, openly sneer at the traditional values of western civilization and promise to destroy them. Believers in democracy have no ground on which to stand in arguing their case against the Fascist.

What students of communication psychology have learned about the critical interaction between articulated opinion and inner attitude supports this view. So, too, it seems to me, do the gradual but significant changes that have been taking place in Communist policies throughout the world. One *can* talk peace and plot war. But the process puts at least one more obstacle in the path of aggression.

Perhaps another way of saying all this is that, whatever the case with nations, the gap between word and deed can be for individuals the real measure of hope. When I lie about my intentions I may simply be trying to deceive and exploit others. But perhaps I am doing something a bit more complex. Perhaps I am giving others a kind mortgage on my future, an earnest of something better to come.

George Dennis O'Brien in his great little book, God And The New Haven Railway, *applies this line of thought to the deathbed repentance in a very persuasive way.*

The Limits of Liberation

January, 1973

Call it pedantry if you wish, but I have begun to have some serious reservations about the current popularity of the word "liberation." First we had Black Liberation, then Women's Liberation and now Gay Liberation. And in its verb form the concept was used not too long ago to describe everything from the occupation of a dean's office to the sexual integration of the library toilets.

Now, in the words of one of my favorite non-heroes, let me make one thing perfectly clear. The substance of the concerns which march under this banner commands my attention and respect. Our society has left undone much that it ought to have done and done that which it ought not to have done and is pretty unhealthy. Many segments of it have every right to stand up and demand redress of grievances.

Nor would I deny that there is a sense in which the use of the word "liberation" in its strictest definition is fully justified. Women and minority groups still suffer from gross forms of repressive coercion. Some are imposed by external social influences, others by internalized patterns shaped during centuries of second-class citizenship. The appropriate response to many of these is the demand for *freedom.*

In some respects, however, the effort to cluster a complex of claims under the heading of liberation is both strategically unwise and socially counterproductive. Many of the changes that are being demanded really have more to do with justice, dignity, opportunity, equality and security than with freedom. Black people, for example, want a greater share of political and economic power, better schools for their children, a sense of ethnic identity and a number of basic rights which can only *loosely* be classified as liberation.

Women are struggling to break psychological stereotypes and open opportunities which will grow not so much out of extended freedom as from a more fully human self-image. Those who call themselves "gay" want to be included in the human community and not regarded with socially encouraged revulsion. This involves more than mere liberation.

It is true, of course, that the term liberation is frequently used in spite of an acknowledged inadequacy. It has a splendid ring to it and fits neatly into the American tradition. One should not be surprised that it has become a kind of umbrella under which diverse and sometimes contradictory interests are gathered.

But social movements tend to become both the victims and the captives of their language. And I discern two ways in which this is happening to those who exploit "liberation."

First, the use of the word confuses many honest people. Those whose minds operate in relatively linear fashion often find it hard to square the specific demands of militant crusaders with the theme of liberation. It may seem to them that their black neighbors who ask for compensatory social goals and women who campaign for an end to media exploitation of dehumanized sex are "going too far." In other words, the notion of liberation sets psychological boundaries to what such groups are expected to fight for. When they push beyond those implied limits they are likely to be accused of hypocrisy or extremism. A more precise vocabulary might have a salutary impact upon public judgments.

Second, in an era much given to privatistic irresponsibility the concept of liberation as the answer to injustice has unfortunate reverberations. It seems to suggest that the crises of our time can be met by finding out who has the key and compelling him or her to unlock the door and turn us loose. It encourages bitter ad hominem arguments where dispassionate analysis is called for. And it threatens to identify liberation with the "me-mine" recidivism of right wing reactionaries.

I want to contend that the need of our age is not for separation into interest groups glaring with hostility at something called the "establishment." It is, rather, for some well-balanced view of human beings in their social context, men and women able to relate creatively to one another regardless of racial, ethnic or national differences.

Well, I am not persuaded that the rhetoric of social dissent will change in response to this fragile appeal. But I am convinced that it is important for those of us who deal so frequently with words as a means of grace to understand the ways in which they can limit as well as serve our ministries.

What I failed to see when this was written is that the "me-mine" psychology may *be more essential than accidental in Liberation Theology.*

An Altar Ego

March, 1973

During the past six months I have heard seven sermons preached about that unpleasantness between Abraham and Isaac in the land of Moriah. And their net effect has been to demonstrate once again the great gulf that exists between most ministers and their congregations. Nothing reveals more clearly the dehumanizing influence of a theological education than the ability of the clergy to pietize this frightful story.

Countless times in Marquand Chapel and in neighborhood churches, I have seen honest souls drench the pulpit with sweat as they strove to persuade their listeners that there is something spiritually edifying about Abraham's willingness to sacrifice his son on the altar of God. And I must admit that most congregations are genteel in their reactions. They refrain from throwing hymnbooks, vomiting on the floor or otherwise expressing what they feel. But the hostile vibes that they give off would, if properly harnessed, wipe out a division of Russian tanks or even depress Hubert Humphrey, briefly.

Now I do not often take the side of lay piety against the counsels of theologians. In fact, one of my serious reservations about the Reformation is its tendency to encourage the uninformed to argue with their betters over matters of faith and morals. In the case of Abraham vs. Isaac, however, my heart is right out there in the pews.

This is not because I am irresistably drawn to the lad Isaac who probably had a smart mouth and deserved what he almost got. (And when one has been travelling for three days on a crowded donkey with a small boy it takes no great excess of piety to be willing to murder him!)

No. My problem with this tale is that it makes a kind of distinction between the *form* of faith on the one hand and the *substance* of faith on the other. In the great philosophical debate about whether God wills the good because it is good or the good is good because God wills it, this incident comes down thumpingly on the side of the latter proposition. Whatever God appears to demand is by definition good, without regard to where it fits into the *overall structure* of the divine self-disclosure. If God says, slaughter the Amalekites, every last one of them, this primitive savagery must be rationalized by piety. If God says, murder your son, the foul deed is made righteousness.

Such a view of things, you see, makes faith radically legalistic, and in so doing traps all of us like so many rats in a maze of juridical theology. Grace, mercy, freedom . . . these things become formal categories devoid of persuasive content.

What lay men and women feel instinctively, which is hid from the wise and just, is that absolute obedience to the divine will is impossible for finite creatures. Human beings cannot look upon the face of God and remain truly human. Nor can we transcend radically our humanity in the search for truth. Those who attempt it are very likely to come up with an act as loathesome in its ruthless brutality as Abraham's effort to sacrifice Isaac or Adolf Hitler's undertaking to build a new Europe on the bodies of "lesser" races.

To claim the ability to discern the will of God outside the context of those relative concerns and values which make up history is to claim a dangerous equality with God. For Abraham to say, I *know* that God wants me to do what every decent feeling I have rejects, is blasphemy. Not because it slanders God. But because it exalts Abraham. It asserts his ability to know God above, beyond, and in *contradiction* to the facts of human experience. It claims for this finite creature the power to transcend and even negate his personal history and deny its most precious relationships. To affirm Abraham's obedience at the cost of all that makes him human is to lay a foundation for the most destructive kind of pride.

The Christian believes that in Jesus Christ we have seen the form and the substance of the divine will united in history Those to whom this grace has been given can never reject it, even to cope with a difficult text.

When this one was expanded into a Battell Chapel sermon it sent several Campus Crusader Yalies storming out of the church in high dudgeon.

41

A Raft of Possibilities
May, 1973

When I was an undergraduate at the University of Michigan a few years ago, the Episcopal Student Fellowship used to hold spring picnics at a lake near Ann Arbor. They were pleasant occasions replete with the usual campfire cookery and the kind of boy-girl fooling around on the beach that could easily qualify for a G rating these days but which was pretty racy stuff then.

One warm Saturday afternoon I swam out to the raft, heaved myself topside, and found that I was alone with a lissome creature who had only recently joined the blessed company of the apostolic. She looked me over in what was then called "a brazen manner" and said, "Gee, you're not really as stodgy as you seem with your clothes on."

Well, she was wrong. I *was* really as stodgy as I seemed with my clothes on. When the real Bill Muehl stood up he was wearing a coat, a tie, pants, and shoes. And probably even a vest. The slender tanned boy in swimming briefs, water and sunlight dripping from golden curls (I said it was a few years ago, didn't I!) was the illusion.

Fortunately the young woman had a veritable vocation to remedy such disjunctions and in short order . . . but that's another story.

The experience dramatized vividly for me the danger of a reductionist view of human nature, the notion that the *real* man or woman is the creature stripped of everything that might conceivably be regarded as artifice.

Over the years I have come to have a professional interest in this matter because of the problem which it poses for preaching. Again and again when I try to get a student to speak with greater vitality in the pulpit he or she protests that such a change would be "unnatural." It is commonly supposed that the only sincere form of human speech is that which puts a maximum number of listeners to sleep in the shortest possible time. I have even had student preachers refuse to speak loudly enough to be heard beyond the fifth pew, because such an effort smacked of artifice.

But this attitude has implications more serious than the handicaps which it may impose upon the clergy. It can confuse the judgments which we make of one another in very serious respects.

From time to time some member of the community, one who had always seemed the soul of respectability, kicks over the traces and shocks us to the core. After twenty years of successful marriage he or she gets involved in an extra-marital dalliance. Or caps a long and useful career at the bank by borrowing illegally from the till.

Too frequently the response to such a revelation is, "So that's the kind of person he is!" Or "All these years she had us fooled and only now do we find out what's inside. What dupes we've been!"

This is the same kind of reductionism, isn't it? Years of faithfulness are seen to have been so much sham. All the thoughtful and responsible acts are forgotten. And every memory is poisoned by what is taken to be the "revelatory" moment.

There are, I am sure, many reasons for this sort of thinking. But one of them is obviously a pop version of the doctrine of original sin. Since human beings are corrupt at the core, goes the argument, then they are most truly themselves when they are at their worst. And, conversely, the better they appear the greater the degree of their hypocrisy. So the preacher is most sincere when he or she is most distressingly inept. And politicians reveal their "true colors" only when they fall from grace.

But that is much too easy, isn't it? We are fearfully complex creatures. The fumbling incompetence and erratic morality are real. But so is inspired eloquence and years of faithful love. A large part of what it means to be truly free is to see a great many possibilities as equally authentic.

What does it say about our time that three personal friends thanked me for having written this with them quite clearly in mind?

Rhetoric, Riots and Reaction

November, 1973

No one with an ounce of sense is likely to be taken in by Jeb Magruder's pose as the William Sloane Coffin of the Nixon administration. For one thing, had Bill Coffin wanted information from the files of the Democratic National Committee, he would have gone after it more in the style of Dirty Harry than in the myopic marauding of Mr. Magoo. The fact that Magruder professes to see no distinction between surreptitious entry with larcenous intent and publicly proclaimed civil disobedience is one more evidence that the bright young men of the G.O.P. have a way of disappointing us.

But having said that, one must in fairness admit that the White House spokesmen who make such comparisons, however faulty in their logic, have an interesting psychological point to score.

The atmosphere of campus disorders, urban riots and massive demonstrations in the latter half of the sixties was unnerving for a great many people. And the rhetoric which accompanied it did little to moderate its impact on the public psyche. Acts which taken in themselves were well within the bounds of legitimate dissent, even characteristically American, seemed pretty frightening when they came simultaneously or in rapid sequence and were orchestrated with words and gestures ordinarily reserved for sermons on Armageddon.

It was obvious that in some cases the aim of protest movements was to cause panic, to shake foundations, to imply that at any moment anger might break through into violence. Nor does it stray from the truth to admit that an element of irrationality was deliberately injected into the more dramatic confrontations. Some New Left leaders and black militants effectively exploited what Norman Maier's experiments with rats taught us about frustration by making such extreme or inconsistent demands that they could not even be discussed rationally. And the public was often made to feel that it had fallen into a low-budget madhouse.

We have every right to be indignant that our nation's top men stooped to tactics such as those involved in Watergate and the Ellsberg break-ins. And I will gladly sign any reasonable petition demanding resignations and/or prosecutions. But we become guilty of our own brand of hyprocrisy when we pretend to be unable to understand the psychology of those who perpetrated such indecencies.

Social order is a fragile thing. What establishes and upholds it is not so much a collection of documents or an aggregation of policemen. It is a spirit that has been called "civility." The assumption is that there are limits to how roughly the game is going to be played, even by scoundrels. It is constructively visible in current efforts to civilize political campaigning. But in perverse form it can also be seen in the tendency of the underworld to set boundaries beyond which even outlaws must not go. (Ask prison officials how long a child murderer will last, if put in an open cell block.)

When the atmosphere of civility is polluted by more disorder than ordinary people can tolerate, no matter how badly provoked, no matter how well motivated, social inhibitions tend to deteriorate and men and women at all levels of life feel liberated to use chicanery and violence for their own purposes. We have had ample opportunities to see how this happens during wartime when otherwise decent men commit fearful atrocities and many patterns of responsible morality fall before over-stimulated emotions.

I am not suggesting now that dissent be stifled or that people of conscience silence their inner voices. My concern is for a more realistic appraisal of consequences in the selection of tactics. When one deliberately scares the hell out of people, one should be prepared for the possibility that they will over-react and behave like cornered rats. And perhaps we should display a little less self-righteousness in judging those who took the rhetoric of dissent at face value.

Several recent books by ex-campus-radicals testify to their belated discovery of this fact. And a couple of them acknowledge that their main aim was an early version of terrorism.

The Wages of Sin Are — Too High

January, 1974

Many years ago Pitrim Sorokin, the Harvard sociologist, became disenchanted with college undergraduates. They were, he opined, intellectual lightweights, devoid of serious purpose, and given too much to the frivolities of the world.

Unlike some who level such indictments Sorokin had a solution to propose. It consisted of a radically new form of college entrance examination. Let each candidate, he suggested, be locked for twenty-four hours in a room provided with luscious food, strong drink and voluptuous women. And let him be required to abstain from the enjoyment of any of these delights. Anyone who passed the test would be granted immediate admission to the college of his choice. The others would be banished into outer darkness.

The Sorokin Plan was given wide circulation in the press and stirred up quite a bit of discussion, especially in the groves of academe. Reactions to it differed. But there was a clear consensus to the effect that such a procedure would undoubtedly do more to stimulate college applications than even unlimited scholarships. "Oh, for the privilege of flunking that test!" was the watchword of the week.

The day after the proposal hit the headlines I had a conference with one of my instructors and asked him what he thought of it. His first response was to grin wryly and say, "I wouldn't trust anyone who could pass that kind of test." But then he went on in a more serious vein. "You know, Muehl, the basis of all morality is the prudence not to walk into such a room in the first place."

At the time, entangled as I was in the toils of an adolescent moral heroism, that answer seemed to me an obvious cop-out. The good Christian, I reasoned, will stand firm in spite of all. To avoid what moralists call "the occasions for sin" struck me as an unworthy legalism, something beneath the dignity of the dedicated believer.

Then I encountered Reinhold Niebuhr and the implications of human finitude. And I recalled a boyhood experience in Kentucky.

For one frustrating year I was a member of the Prestonia Midgets basketball team. The basic mechanics of the game gave me little trouble. But I was grievously lacking in what the coach called "a competitive spirit." Month after month I sat on the bench trying to understand the meaning of that phrase. The more people tried to explain it to me, the more it seemed to be just a disguised form of cheating, playing something halfway between basketball and soccer.

Finally, in the last month of the season, the coach gave me one more chance, and I went onto the floor determined to show lots of "competitive spirit." In a little less than five minutes I was expelled from the game for having committed four personal fouls!

Someone has said that the truest test of the character of any society is the way it treats its least powerful members. That is undoubtedly one true test. But I want to suggest another, i.e. the way it treats its ablest members, the temptations to which it regularly subjects its achievers, the degree to which a society counts on moral heroism to keep the system reasonably honest.

America sometimes seems to have adopted Sorokin's view of human nature and applied it far beyond the admissions office. We offer fabulous rewards to men and women who can operate effectively in the twilight zone between honesty on the one hand and dishonesty on the other, between public service and public betrayal.

There is a sense in which we harness some of the most dangerous of human emotions and then count on the perfect functioning of internal moral governors to keep people from doing what the dynamics of wealth and status propose.

It is true that much of our material affluence reflects the abuse of the poor and powerless. But it also represents a calculated and cynical exploitation of the strong and successful. We fatten on the sweat and wasted limbs of children. And no less on the bleeding ulcers and broken marriages of the "man most likely to succeed."

A God who sees the fall of the smallest sparrow may judge the one crime as seriously as the other.

I continue to find it ironic that many people who herald the wideness of God's mercy in dealing with social outcasts are rigidly legalistic in their reactions to white collar crime.

The Gentleman As Tyrant

May, 1974

At the close of World War II the theater critics of New York City were thrown into something of a tizzy by Jean Anouilh's version of the Greek drama *Antigone*. This play, you will recall, poses the classic conflict between freedom and authority. Antigone, the protagonist, is determined to bury the body of her brother, executed for crimes against the state. Creon, the tyrant, has ruled that the corpse must be left exposed to the elements and public contempt.

What bothered the drama critics was the *reasonableness* of Creon. He did not talk the way tyrants are supposed to talk. He granted the propriety of Antigone's sentiments and explained his own position in terms of sound social policy. He neither screamed invective nor foamed at the mouth but spoke, rather, as Marse Robert might have done to explain the Late Unpleasantness to an elderly Richmond librarian.

Having just emerged from a war in which oppression was incarnate in two strutting and demented dictators, the journalists in question felt troubled by the sanity and temperate utterance of Creon's convictions. How could tyranny be portrayed in so soft a light? Some blamed Katherine Cornell, who played Antigone, for not rendering *her* part with greater force. Others insisted that Sir Cedric Hardwicke, as Creon, had been given all the best lines. The battle raged for months, continuing in the pages of avant-garde magazines long after it had ceased to rate newspaper space.

I built a couple of sermons around the controversy and then forgot about it for a while. But echoes of the incident have begun to disturb me of late. The violent disruption of an intended visit to Yale by General William Westmoreland a few years ago and more recent efforts to block a campus debate between Roy Innis of C.O.R.E. and William Shockley, the self-proclaimed geneticist, suggest that a great many people today suffer from the myopia which afflicted the New York drama critics. They cannot see tyranny beneath their own "good" reasons for suppressing freedom of discussion.

The danger inherent in such a situation was brought home to me in my own student days when a group of us wanted to have Earl Browder, the Communist Party candidate for President, speak on our campus. The Commander of the local American Legion Post breathed threats and slaughter. State legislators stood in line at the microphones to demand that we be expelled from college as a salutary example to the youth of the nation. Conservative newspapers predicted the imminent demise of democracy. And a few Interfraternity Council officers muttered darkly about bloodying some noses. None of these pressures deterred us.

But then one day an associate dean called us to his office. He was a great guy. Students loved him for the right reasons. He had fought our battles, individual and collective, at some risk to his own career. And several of us owed him for personal favors. He champed on his briar pipe, expressed sympathy for our position, scoffed at the notion that Browder's coming to campus would threaten the Republic. And then very nicely asked us to cancel the invitation. The university's budget, it seemed, was being mauled by the state legislature. Some flannel-mouthed rural demagogues had set about using the Browder issue as an excuse for massive cuts in our appropriations. All sorts of necessary and progressive programs would be destroyed, if reaction won the field.

This was the appeal that really shook us. How do you turn down a friend, especially when he states his case in terms of values which both of you cherish?

It is easy to recognize oppression when it marches jack-booted through the streets. But can we see it behind the anguished countenance of a young person enraged by carnage in Viet Nam? Or in the eyes of blacks infuriated by racial stereotypes? If we cannot, one of our most important civil liberties may be down the drain.

It says something frightening about the late sixties and early seventies that I was complimented by several people for my "courage" in writing this one.

An Ounce of Prevention

November, 1974

I am told that a store in downtown New Haven displays a sign denying entrance to anyone under sixteen who is not accompanied by an adult. Since nothing conspicuously pornographic occurs on the premises, the obvious intent of the prohibition is to discourage shoplifting. Groups of teen-agers have in recent years taken to roaming through business enterprises with larcenous enthusiasm. And the amount of merchandise which disappears annually into their capacious pockets can spell the difference between viability and disaster for small merchants.

The sign suggests a rise in the sheer volume of petty theft in our society. But it is symptomatic of something else as well. Something which in long run terms may be more troublesome. For what the store owner in question is doing is substituting preventive for punitive measures in dealing with crime. He is saying that since we cannot detect, apprehend and punish thieves, we must bar certain high-crime categories of persons from places where they may constitute a threat to property.

That in itself worries me. But it is merely one outward and visible sign of something even more disturbing, i.e. the widespread substitution of surveillance and infiltration for more traditional methods of law enforcement.

During one of the hearings growing out of the Watergate scandal a government agent testified to the increasing use of secret agents and paid informers in various anti-war and political protest groups. They are necessary, he argued, because public opinion will no longer tolerate harsh treatment of those who engage in acts of public protest. So long as the police felt free, he went on, to act with effective brutality in quelling riots, they really did not need to be alerted in advance to plans for mass demonstrations. When trouble broke out they could simply wade in with clubs, fire hoses, tear gas and attack dogs to disperse the crowd in short order.

When, however, strict limits are placed by courts upon the degree of force that may be used in any situation strategy becomes more important than weaponry. And the development of sound strategy requires among other things reconnaissance, advance notice of what impends. It becomes necessary to predict where disruptive acts are likely to occur, so that steps can be taken to contain them with minimum violence. And it also becomes desirable to prevent such occurrences, even if this means planting agents whose job it is to disorganize protest groups by discrediting their leaders, provoking factional strife and engaging in what have come to be called "dirty tricks." Far better, this reasoning runs, to sow discord among members of the New Left or Veterans Against Viet Nam than to have to confront a well-organized group of these protesters in the middle of Main Street.

This phenomenon cannot be dismissed as merely one more unpleasant side-effect of Richard Nixon's need–to–know. There are instructive historical parallels which imply that something more significant is at work. It has been reliably reported that as the absolute power of monarchies in eighteenth century France and twentieth century Russia declined, the influence of the secret police in both of these countries increased greatly. When you can no longer behead the opposition you must stab it in the back!

Most Christians vibrate pleasantly to the idea that the prevention of crime is better than its detection and punishment. And to the degree that this means eradicating the poverty and injustice from which much crime arises the principle deserves the support of the wise and just. But in our zeal to inhibit stop-and-search, detain-and-question, convict-and-punish approaches to law and order we may be inviting something a lot worse. The impulses of unsophisticated compassion are not always the best basis for social policy.

There are things worse than being punished. One of them is to be denied the freedom to do anything wrong.

This one brought accusations that I had become a "law and order liberal." To these I plead nolo contendere.

Let Us Pray!

January, 1975

One Sunday years ago I attended the eleven o'clock service of worship at a small-town church in Pennsylvania. As I entered the usher handed me several sheets of paper covered with what was obviously financial data. And I noticed that a slide projector and screen had been set up in the center aisle.

When the time came for the sermon the pastor announced that since very few of those present would appear at the Annual Meeting, he was going to give the congregation a detailed analysis of the budget for the next year. And he proceeded to do this in a manner reminiscent of Robert Benchley's "The Treasurer's Report."

That incident brought into focus something that I had begun to suspect somewhat earlier in my career, i.e. that a major reason for the decline of effective preaching is the tendency of Protestant Christians to overburden the sermon. As it has become more and more difficult to gather the faithful at any other hour or occasion in the week, ministers have come to depend increasingly upon the "sermon" to carry the total communication task of the church.

As a result proclamation of the gospel is often subordinated to a great many other laudable institutional purposes. And the vitality of preaching has suffered.

Now it is undoubtedly important for the congregation to be informed about the bishop's most recent concern, the sad state of the heating plant, the shortage of Sunday School teachers, and the treachery of the parsonage plumbing. But the effort to carry on such discussions as sermons puts a knife at the throat of preaching.

More recently, it has seemed to me, the whole Sunday morning service has been threatened with an extension of the same affliction. One observes among the younger clergy the assumption that anything that Christians ought to do together is appropriate as *worship.* This misapprehension has, of course, a long and painful history, as anyone familiar with children's pageants can attest. I am not sure who first got the idea that the place to demonstrate the thespian talents of our offspring is in the chancel at eleven o'clock on Sunday, but whoever it was has gained a host of latter-day adherents.

Today the range of activities which innovative souls wish to have defined as public worship is almost limitless. And most congregations are getting inured to the presence of loudspeakers, amplified guitars, overhead projectors, tape recorders, balloons and trained seals before the altar of the Lord. Nor are we greatly dismayed when exhorted to clap, dance, hug, kiss, and pinch one another as modes of common prayer.

But it seems to me that some of what is regarded as liturgical "enrichment" reflects the spirit that has so badly damaged preaching, the unwillingness to expect Christians to give more than one hour a week to their church. Of course we should have opportunities to see and participate in religious dance, drama, multi-media presentations and a heartwarming variety of opportunities for fellowship. But when we insist upon trying to cram all of these experiences into the chancel between eleven and twelve o'clock on Sunday, we threaten the integrity of worship and make a damning statement about the fullness of our religious commitments.

It would be far better, I am persuaded, to recognize that a

satisfying Christian life needs to be nourished and instructed in many ways. There is much besides worship that we ought to be doing together in our churches to express both the depth of our spiritual need and the richness of God's grace. If we face this fact and respond imaginatively to it, we may be able to prevent the Sunday morning service from becoming a circus rather than a sacrament.

There is, of course, another extreme, i.e. filling the service with so many rediscovered liturgical riches that the trained seals would be suffocated by the incense!

Grace in a Maze

November, 1975

The tennis courts have been resurfaced. Just about the time the Divinity School opened for business this fall an exceeding great host of workers descended upon our play space and rehabilitated it. The courts now look so professional that one is a bit embarrassed to go upon them in anything but the traditional whites or television blues. The local Jimmy Connerses and Chris Everts are in the Seventh Heaven. And a few Bobby Riggses can also be seen serving invisible aces to non-existent Billy Jean Kings with quite imaginary tennis balls.

What makes this so remarkable is the fact that Yale University is experiencing a serious financial crunch. Substantive programs are being reviewed, personnel cutbacks have become real threats and new projects have had to be quietly shelved.

There is no doubting any of this. The economic problems of private universities are not mere figments of zealous fundraisers' imaginations. Inflation and the stock market slump have hurt academe seriously.

But throughout the university one comes upon evidence that the heavy hand of thrift has not been able to squeeze all the joy out of education. Little luxuries still turn up here and there for which no financially persuasive defense can be made. An occasional bottle of red wine on the undergraduates' dinner tables, new sod on a college courtyard lawn, an augmented symphony orchestra and resurfaced tennis courts. (Paid for, incidentally, out of the Athletic Department budget.)

All this reflects what I have come to think of as the grace of bureaucracy. In any large, complex organization there is always a good bit of slippage between the front office and the stockroom. Long after stern orders have gone forth from the throne to cut expenditures to the bone and reduce all of life to a gray monotone, a kind of inertia generated in more affluent days keeps producing the kinds of artifacts and programs which have been interdicted. Not because some rebellious spirit is determined to defy the mood of the times, but because the "word" never really *reaches* everyone. Plans get made and implemented long after the authorization for them has been revoked.

At the end of World War II, for example, the English discovered that in spite of austerity and total defense mobilization eccentric little shops hidden in the twisting lanes of London or out among country hedgerows had gone on producing and selling things which were quite useless to the war effort and required significant quantities of both labor and scarce materials. No one had thought to tell people not to eat the daisies. So life amid the ruins of modern war was made a little more human by bureaucratic foul-ups.

In more somber terms we hear stories from Germany which suggest that even the total power of Adolf Hitler was not able to overcome the Teutonic addiction to "correct" paperwork. Proscribed persons sometimes managed to escape their persecutors because the proper forms were not filled out in time to allow their apprehension. And it has been reported that the prisoners in one small and obscure concentration camp continued to eat relatively well right up to the day of liberation, because an unrevoked authorization kept directing carloads of potatoes to them long after that commodity had become scarce among civilians.

We hear a lot of justified complaining about bureaucracy. And its blighting timidity does cause a good deal of human inconvenience and suffering. But let's give the devil his or her due. The inertia generated by the bureaucratic mentality sometimes serves to balance the panic responses of policymakers in times of crisis. Given human corruption and the advanced technology of self-destruction, it is entirely possible that we may one day be saved from nuclear holocaust by someone's failure to issue the fatal order in triplicate.

Until then, tennis anyone?

This one was posted on the bulletin board of the University Secretary's office for some time. (Luke XVI, 9)

The Politics of Paving Blocks

January, 1976

In the days immediately following the Russian overthrow of the "liberal" Dubjec regime in Czechoslovakia a Czech and a Hungarian were discussing the political disasters which had engulfed their respective homelands.

"But we resisted," the Hungarian said. "We fought until we were overcome. You did nothing."

"What could we do?" the Czech asked. "We had no weapons with which to fight."

"Neither did we," was the response. "But we used whatever came to hand. We tore limbs off trees, threw bottles filled with gasoline and pulled up paving blocks to make barricades against their tanks."

"Ah," said the Czech, "would that we could have done the same. But, you see, in Prague it is against the law to tear up paving blocks."

One would like to regard that anecdote as simply a comment upon the infirmities of a people who have known too much tyranny. Who is so foolish as to suppose that you can fight revolutions without breaking laws?

Well, increasing numbers of modern Americans to start with.

The other night I watched a television program in which two leaders of the women's movement in the United States were being interviewed about the progress of liberation. At one point they were asked to explain the failure of a recent one-day strike by working women intended to demonstrate their importance to the economy. Why had so few women taken part in that act of defiance?

Indignantly the spokeswomen responded. It was the fault of the employers. Many of them had threatened to dock female employees' wages or force them to make up lost time if they took that day off. Naturally the victims of such inhuman pressure dropped out of the strike program. How could they be expected to do otherwise?

During the campus disruptions of the sixties many young people of both sexes often seemed stunned by the discovery that social activism can be costly, even dangerous. On a bus coming back from one Washington demonstration, I heard a graduate student complain bitterly that a thoughtless judge had jailed him for three days following another protest action, "even though he knew damned well that I had my orals on Monday!" And it was not uncommon to have the summons to close down the academic establishment suddenly muted by the realization that such a procedure might result in delayed bursary checks or diminished course credit.

People raised on game theory seem often to suppose that the establishment is bound by the rules of sportsmanship to pick up the tab for its own dismemberment. Or that political bosses, if denounced strongly enough, will cut their own throats and then apologize for getting blood on the carpet.

I knew a number of militant Communists when I was in college. Many of them were thoroughly reprehensible people, pathological liars and victims of a rigid ideological commitment. But they had about them an admirable and gutsy realism. They were not intimidated by the law against tearing up paving blocks. And they understood that you cannot set fire to the old homestead and then expect sympathy from Dad because your

Teddy Bear gets singed!

Are you aware that the application of historical parallels to contemporary problems is "insensitive?" I learned it the hard way.

Kahlil Gibran Did Not Die for Our Sins

March, 1976

Recently I read somewhere the lament of a young man whose parents had obviously been pestering him to make firm decisions about his future. "My father keeps asking me *what* I want to be," he complained, "but why do I have to be *something*? Why can't I just be?"

Well, as a rhetorical gambit used in an all too familiar context the question has much to commend it. We can easily imagine a chagrined old man skulking off to the Union League Club or some other establishment lair to lick his wounds in humiliation while pondering the wisdom of youth. It was a good put-down.

But as a serious inquiry about life it shows a lamentable ignorance of what it means to be human. To live in history is to be *somebody* who *does* things. Not necessarily in the sense that the young man's father may have had in mind, i.e. to be a person of substance who shapes the course of great events. But to recognize the fact that each of us is fully human to the degree that he or she accepts the particularities of time, place and action.

This elementary fact about life was brought home to me many years ago in one of those college sex lectures that have since been replaced by laboratory experiments. Margaret Mead had spoken at length about the various patterns which one finds in male-female relating in different times and places. She made it quite clear that life-long monogamy is by no means a given.

When the audience had broken up into buzz groups one young buzzer could hardly control his impatience to ask the convener, a Lutheran campus pastor, a challenging question. "Since marriage as we know it may not even exist a couple hundred years from now (Boy, was his timing off!), why should I accept it as the only appropriate mode of sexual relating?"

The pastor thought for a moment and then replied, "Because you don't live a couple hundred years from now. *You* live *now*."

The fellow who had asked the question was not greatly persuaded by that answer. But since I had recently discovered Reinhold Niebuhr, the words had a ring of familiar truth to them. Upon reflection it seemed clear to me that I had always been most vulnerable to corruption when I tried to escape the mundane and act in terms of abstract possibilities rather than concrete fact. There was something about the sights, sounds, smells and texture of reality which kept calling me back to accountability, and a quality to my fantasies which encouraged irresponsibility.

A middle-aged German who had been in his youth a member of the Elite Corps of the Nazi S.S. once reminisced for television about his experience. "We were imbued with the vision of a master race that would lead humanity out of the painful, materialistic present into a bright new future. And blinded by the brightness of that dream, we drove Jews into gas ovens and performed cruel experiments on living human subjects."

We Christians make much of what we like to call the "scandal of particularity," the revelation of the eternal in the temporal, in specific historical events and personalities. But sometimes we seem to suppose that to be *redeemed* is to put that scandal behind us and to be able to respond to God's love in ways that are *not* conditioned by the relativities of time, place and action. And when we do this, whether in matters of personal morality or public policy, we discover the hard way what the Bible makes so clear, that those who seek to transcend their humanity inevitably fall far below it.

One of the reasons that I have so much trouble getting our students to speak loudly enough in Chapel is that many of them developed their interest in religion in college, when they sat in a circle on the floor in someone's dormitory room, put a candle in the center and read The Prophet *to one another. This leads to the equation of "spirituality" with solemn murmurs.*

A Second Thought

May, 1976

From time to time *The Christian Century* invites some distinguished theologian to write an article entitled, "How My Mind Has Changed." These essays describe the ways in which the author has revised his or her ideas on important matters over the years. I have waited in vain for one of those invitations. At last my patience has worn thin. Revealing a flexibility which does not always appear on the surface of my personality, I take this occasion to announce that my mind *has* changed on a few subjects. And I propose to reveal one of them right now. (Eat your heart out, Martin Marty!)

In a valiant effort to combat the nefarious pietism which for so long infected Protestant social thought, I used to write and say that it is a serious mistake to base political judgments on the quality of a candidate's private life, i.e. personal morality. I would, I have sometimes declared, vote for a drunken adulterer or a housebroken baboon pledged to the support of progressive causes rather than for a model of virtue who has the wrong attitudes on current social issues. And in practice I have more than lived up to my preachments, even choosing on occasion to waive the toilet training.

I am still willing to support the major thrust of that argument. God is as much concerned with the objective consequences of human actions as with the character of the actor. Men and women who stand for humane and responsible public policy deserve our support, even though their domestic lives may leave something to be desired. (Or *nothing* to be desired, depending on whose point of view you're taking.)

Over the years, however, I have become less cavalier about neatly separating public and private postures. Or to put it another way, it now seems to me that my original position must be qualified in two significant respects.

First, in a society whose moral compass seems more and more to be fixed upon the life-styles of prestigious public figures, one ought to have some reservations about raising to high office those whose values are at marked variance from one's own. It would be absurd to suggest that recent revelations about the sexual proclivities of some national leaders will in exactly nine months produce a bumper crop of illegitimate offspring. But it would be equally foolish to suppose that the moral ethos is not in dramatic ways influenced by such disclosures.

Only the hopelessly naive will argue that personal value judgments are made by pure reason operating in a socio-cultural vacuum. Diverse pressures and permissions flow in upon us from every direction. And the difference between interpersonal responsibility and cruel exploitation is often based on nothing more exalted than the laudable desire to avoid public censure. The examples set by those in positions of authority are among the many powerful influences bearing upon the shape of the human future.

Second, it is by no means clear to me that there is no connection whatever between faithfulness to a marriage vow, let us say, and fidelity in the discharge of a sane foreign policy or the formulation of sound welfare programs. Obviously one cannot prove a connection between political miscalculations and a roving eye. But given what we have begun to learn about the complex interaction of psychological patterns which seem on the surface to be unrelated, I am unwilling to compartmentalize public and private behavior as I once did.

Responsibility may be a seamless garment. The arrogance which leads one to suppose that he or she can move with blithe insouciance across a field of quite casual relationships, flouting the traditions which guide and govern lesser folk, is very likely to reveal itself in subtle and not so subtle style when more massive issues are at stake. A weakness for the bottle is relatively harmless politically where matters of budget and tariffs are concerned. It can be a nasty business in one who sleeps with a finger on the ultimate button.

Developments at the Democratic National Convention this summer may make me want to eat those words. If they do, I pray for the grace to feel at least a touch of indigestion.

I broke into a Christian Century *editorial with this one, long before Senator Gary Hart enhanced its relevance.*

Long Live the King!
January, 1977

Richard Niebuhr once accused me of having what he called "a low doctrine of the church and a high doctrine of the state." The charge came during a discussion in which I had argued vociferously that God is as active in the secular processes of history as in the explicitly "spiritual" commitments of human beings. There are social values, I insisted, which may reflect the divine will at a given moment more fully than competing religious claims. And these must be protected against ecclesiastical presumption.

I have been stirred to remember that conversation by a recent series of evenings at the Divinity School in which a mixed audience of academics and townspeople heard presentations on the topic "Faith and Fanaticism." The programs dealt with the growth of contemporary cults such as the Unification Church, the Children of God and the New Testament Missionary Fellowship. Among the speakers were young people who had been in one such group or another, their parents, a psychiatrist, experts on the legal problems of deprogramming and a religious scholar engaged in writing a book on the Unification Church.

Various points of view were presented in both the formal talks and the audience responses. And as I listened to one speaker after another, I was struck by how difficult it is to distinguish in the realm of religion between responsible zeal and exploitive fanaticism.

Many of the charges being leveled against cults today could be directed with equal force against ancient and modern practices in mainline churches. The process of isolating young recruits to protect them against a hostile environment, which causes indignation among us currently, was used for centuries by Roman Catholicism as "cloister." The emotionally intense indoctrination sessions now called "brainwashing" were, until very recently, standard features of the "conversion experience" cherished by Protestant evangelism. And the disruption of family life, which understandably distresses us when it is occasioned by cult loyalties, characterized Christianity's impact upon the ancient world, as Jesus himself warned us it would. ("For I have come to set a man against his father and a daughter against her mother . . . .")

I am not suggesting that there are no important differences between the phenomena associated with Christianity's mainstream and the exotic experiments growing up so rapidly around us today. I *am suggesting* that whatever the differences are, they have become so over a long period of time in which the claims of faith have lived in tension with society's inevitable demand for some degree of rational behavior and canons of judgment. The spiritual quality of contemporary life has been influenced as much by secular necessities as by religious convictions. For God is at work on both sides of that equation. There is a sense in which all pure religion is dangerous. Its private visions and special revelations often lead it to cut ruthlessly across the patterns of life in history and fragment the tenuous unity of the human family. The majestic moments in which it transcends the finite and discloses the eternal threaten the structures of reason and responsibility upon which men and women depend for their survival. The yogi is finally as great a menace to our essential humanity as is the commissar.

Secular society has both a right and an obligation, then, to turn a skeptical eye upon pious mystery and insist that it prove itself within time and under the constant surveillance of that cold scrutiny. Not by repressive measures intended to stifle the spirit. But by asserting vigorously the claims of those common and prudential values upon which the visible human community depends. If it fails to do so and retreats too quickly before the urgency of any cultic revelation, society betrays both its corporate integrity and its individual members. It also fails in its primary obligation to God.

I guess I do have a low doctrine of the church and a high doctrine of the state, because it seems to me that one of the wisest things the people of Israel ever did was to make Samuel give them a king.

What has become of the once passionate, even panicky, preoccupation with cults in the mid-seventies? It seems to have gone the way of the Protestant fear of Christian Science in the twenties.

Where Does It Hurt?

March, 1977

In the small hours of one recent restless night, I listened to a radio program on which several people were discussing narcotics addiction. At one point the chairman of the panel played a taped interview with an addict who made a passionate plea for the decriminalization of drugs. One line kept recurring in his argument: "It don't hurt nobody but the user himself."

In subsequent responses to the tape it came to light that the young man whose views it expressed was at that time in jail. He was accused of having assaulted and robbed an aged storekeeper in order to get money to support his habit and had been convicted twice before of the same offense. Yet he had the temerity to say of his addiction, "It don't hurt nobody but the addict himself."

Few of us would defend that position on narcotics. But it seems to me that an increasing number of people are guilty of promulgating in other ways the fallacy that stands out so glaringly in it. More and more men and women, including religious leaders, are willing to tolerate or support various kinds of dubious behavior on the grounds that they hurt nobody but the one engaged in them. This vulgarized version of contextual ethics is getting quite a play these days.

What this contention overlooks, of course, is that no one can ever say with certainty of *any* human action that its consequences are limited to those who set them in motion. In all but the most isolated instances, what one human being does has subtle ramifications which hurt or help those around him or her in an unending series of concentric circles. Chain smokers who exercise their right to destroy their own lungs poison the air we breathe and stand a fair chance of ending up respiratory basket cases, burdens on the Blue Cross premiums and charity of the rest of us. Suicides acting out the freedom to take their own lives often do immeasurable damage to the lives of others. Even such intimately personal decisions as those involved in birth control and abortion have implications for the commonweal which refute the claims of "personal autonomy." To say that any action is harmless because it does not immediately leave blood on the rug or visible scars on someone's body is manifest nonsense.

It is, I take it, a function of morality to distill inferences for responsible human behavior from a long collective experience, to give each generation the benefit of what other generations have learned about the probable impact upon persons of various kinds of actions and relationships. Precisely because I *cannot know* with any assurance what the real consequences of my own initiatives will be, I am constrained to take seriously the accumulated wisdom of the past. To sweep such experience away in the name of some imagined and omniscient personal sensitivity is at the very least presumptuous.

Do not mistake my point. It is impossible to live even the most exemplary life without inflicting pain. The child struggling to be born hurts its mother. The man or woman who earns a promotion at the office excludes another from that same preferment. The defense of western civilization against Nazi tyranny resulted in the deaths of millions of people. One does not invalidate any enterprise simply by pointing out that it will cause suffering. And there is something sick about that morbid scrupulosity which tries to keep track of all the reverberations of every utterance.

By the same token, however, one cannot *legitimate* any action by the allegation that it harms no one but the actor. All this fallacious argument does is substitute self-righteousness for a chastening sense of corporate guilt. An honest admission that we live by the sacrifices of others will not eliminate that hard fact of life. But it may keep our violence to a minimum and help us direct its use to the optimum human advantage.

A young man who refused to obey the law requiring motorcyclists to wear helmets because it hurt no one but himself to do so is now a hopeless vegetable and a dreadful burden upon his parents.

Bill, son Tim, and Ruth on the Valley Way Trail in
Randolph, New Hampshire about 1950.

Bill taking a moment to practice pipe smoking
on a church outing aboard the "Bob-Lo" Ferry
in the Detroit River, circa 1940.

Son Jon bedding down in an Adirondack lean-to in the mid-1950s.

A University Office of Public Information
photo from the early 1960s — in Bill's pre-
beard incarnation.

Bill and his briefly cherished Corvette in 1959.

Bill, the featured speaker at the 1979 Delaware Episcopal Diocesan dinner, flanked by Dr. Robert B. Scott, and Bill's college roommate, William H. Clark, the retired Bishop of Delaware.

Bill and Ruth ("Chips" to her friends) atop Mount Sugerloaf on a recent Annual Gourmet Hike of the Randolph Mountain Club. Begun by Ruth years ago, this event generates a mountaintop display of vintage wines, exotic dishes and deserts that non-members tend to goggle in amazement.

"Please reserve applause until..." was Bill's opening refrain before dispensing diplomas throughout his four decades — 1949-1989 — as Faculty Marshall.

David Harkness '76, '78, Paul Dahlstrom, and Bill enjoy a Common Room coffee-hour conversation during a recent Winter Convocation.

Right: On break at a United Methodist pastor's conference at Birmingham, Michigan in 1980, are Frank Leineke, Bill, William Ritter '65, and Robert Ward '52.

Bill, in a characteristic pose, lecturing to those Michigan pastors.

Winter 1989 Convocation—Dean Leander Keck; Professor Fred Craddock of the Candler School of Theology at Emory University and the 1989 Beecher Lecturer; Bill, the 1985 Beecher Lecturer; and University Chaplain and Professor Harry Adams, longtime editor of *Reflection*(s).

Bill enjoying himself at the February 1989, Winter Convocation dinner in his honor.

The View from Philistia
November, 1977

I yield to no one in my enthusiasm for the arts and their contribution to the edification of the Christian community. Some of my favorite and oft repeated passages of prose are to be found in the Commager and Hofstadter indictments of the aesthetic poverty of the American Protestant ethos. And on several occasions I have been clutched at the church door by an anxious member of the congregation asking, "But suppose I have no talent at all for painting or poetry?"

In recent years, however, I have been increasingly troubled by the veneration accorded artists of every kind among the more highly educated segments of our society. People who are inclined to lay about them in irreverently critical glee in matters political, economic and religious tend to go all hushed and mushy in the presence of anything that claims to be a "work of art." And the ingenuity with which some achievements in aesthetic obscurantism are exegeted often makes the more convoluted scholastic theologies seem like a McGuffey's Reader by contrast.

Some years ago I worked out a sermon for a university chapel in which I suggested that the arts are as subject to corruption as all other aspects of human experience. The artist, I pointed out, can so distort reality that those who view his or her work may be deceived, even traumatized, by the experience. Is it safe to assume, I asked, that the artist's intentions are always pure? Is it not possible that the sinfulness which leads people to disguise lust as love and irresponsibility as liberation also tempts the artistic spirit to lie about what it perceives in life?

The reaction of the first students to whom I delivered this message dismayed me. Some sneaked out side doors of the chapel to avoid having to greet me. Others stood impatiently in line to denounce so monstrous a thesis. Why, they demanded, did I not confine my preaching to more appropriate topics? In very short order I received many of the brickbats once reserved for sermons urging racial integration.

At the time I was considerably more naive about this matter than I have since become and kept revising the message in order to make my position clear. To no avail. And finally a chaplain's assistant tipped me off en route to the airport one Sunday evening. "Art," he explained, "is just about the only sacred cow allowed to graze safely in the groves of academe. It was the *substance* not the *form* of your thesis that angered them."

Well, there may be many explanations for this special relationship between art and academe. But there is one that makes more sense theologically than any other. The aesthetic enterprise, it seems, is supposed to be one of the most unconditioned of human activities. The true artist responds authentically to things as they are. He or she is not out to make a buck or please a patron but to express what is believed or felt at the deepest level of perception.

To suggest, therefore, that true works of art can be corrupt, not simply in the sense of being sell-outs to the marketplace but as expressions of an essential human perversity, is to make a statement about human sinfulness which our age finds unacceptable. It is to claim that our corruption is not an unwelcome imposition upon the surface of our natures but a reflection of some inherent personal capacity for evil for which no external social influence can be blamed. And the somewhat cynical and often desperate optimism which passes for a doctrine of human nature among us today will hear no such word.

The arts have always enriched the life of faith. But their capacity to do so implies the kind of engagement in human experience which makes purity impossible and judgment inevitable.

This column, expanded into a university chapel sermon, stirred up more congregational anger than any other I have preached in fifty years. Students threatened to boycott services if "that man" was ever invited back. So much for the open mind of the young.

The Specter of the Nose

January, 1978

It happened again the other evening. Some people at a dinner party were cowed into silence by fear of the camel's nose.

They had been discussing the problem of pornography and its effects on the social atmosphere. But before the conversation had gotten very far one of those present began to protest against any legal infringement of the right to promulgate obscene literature and movies. How can one possibly draw a line, he asked, between plain filth and unpopular opinion? The query was put in the style of an insoluble dilemma. And most of those at the table nodded unhappy agreement with its implications. Any move against X-rated films, they were persuaded, presages the inevitable suppression of *The Christian Science Monitor*.

Whatever the merits of particular legislative remedies for the exploitation of sex and violence by the various media, the contention that one cannot "draw a line" between the permissable and the impermissable is sheer nonsense. Drawing such lines is something that individuals and communities do every day, *especially* in the realm of law. Our courts are constantly called upon to decide issues of degree and have little difficulty doing so.

Take, for example, the plea of self-defense in cases involving physical harm to persons. What one may do to prevent anticipated injury depends upon many variables. A fragile octogenerian may use a gun against a threatened assault which a Green Bay Packer

81

would be expected to repel with open hands. And along the spectrum between these extremes there are many way stations at which intermediate degrees of force are allowed. Courts which deal with such cases employ the familiar rule of reason and have great success in doing so.

Or take the area of free speech itself. Most thoughtful men and women accept Justice Holmes's principle that "there is no freedom to cry 'Fire' in a crowded theater." It is commonly supposed to lay down the precise criterion in terms of which government may properly inhibit total freedom of expression.

The fact is that Holmes's famous line is virtually meaningless, so numerous are its ambiguities. How many bodies, for example, must there be in an auditorium to make it a "crowded theater"? And what constitutes the cry of "Fire"? Surely the word itself screamed full voice. But suppose a nervous member of the audience stops a passing usher and says in tones slightly louder than necessary, "I smell smoke"? How many decibels of sound must be present in the articulation of what words in order to summon the Holmes doctrine into operation?

Such questions arise often in cases at law. And it is the function of our judicial system to decide *when* a particular situation involves a degree of malice or negligence sufficient to merit legal reprobation. Our prisons are full of people who simply went one step too far in some course of conduct.

I am sure that most of those who shrink in horror from drawing such lines with respect to pornography are honestly reluctant to set foot upon a path which is not entirely free of peril to human liberty. But I know from personal experience that some of the most vociferous spokespersons for an absolutist position on this subject are motivated less by fear for the Constitution than by a desire to poke a sharp stick into the eye of conventional morality. What more potent weapon can one find for attacking an old enemy than the allegation that its concerns are not only irrelevant but illegal?

The problem of dealing effectively with the degradation of sex in our society is a complicated one. And responsible men and women will differ about whether and how it can be accomplished within the very important framework of free speech. Those who feel called upon to deal with the subject, however, should not allow their discussion to be intimidated by the specter of the camel's nose.

More people than you might believe are unfamiliar with the phrase "the camel's nose under the tent." For their benefit, it suggests that if you ever let the camel get its nose under the tent, the whole beast will soon try to follow it.

Just a Touch of Oregano, Please

April, 1978

During my college years a Jewish friend and I went one evening to a lecture by the local Orthodox rabbi. In the discussion period after the formal address a member of the audience who came from the Reform tradition asked a key question.

"Why should modern Jews continue to accept all the detailed prescriptions of Torah? I acknowledge," he said, "that some of the law still has relevance for our lives. But doesn't Orthodoxy carry the whole thing too far?"

The lecturer's beard bristled piously, his eyes flamed, and he pounced upon the query as though he had been training for years to assail it.

"If 'some' is good," he cried, "surely 'all' is better!"

The audience was so intimidated by his charismatic self-assurance that we nodded dumbly and let the matter drop. But as we left the hall at the close of the program my friend murmured, "I wonder whether he would say the same thing about garlic."

That reminded me of my mother's meatloaf.

Mother was not a gourmet cook, but she did well enough to keep a fussy husband and two spoiled kids reasonably happy. Her best dish was a meatloaf which combined beef and pork in a savory union. The family loved it.

One day, on the advice of a friend, Mother added a touch of oregano to the familiar recipe. We were all delighted with the improvement and lavish in our praise. So the next time around, responsive to the rabbinical psychology, she apparently tripled the amount of oregano that she had used originally. With predictable results. We gagged on the meatloaf, and it was well over a year before any of us could stand even the smell of that particular herb again.

And that brings me to grace. I have become persuaded from listening to generations of struggling young preachers that this theological concept should be regarded as seasoning to the biblical faith rather than as a nourishing item of food in itself. Its effectiveness in accomplishing what it is supposed to accomplish depends, like that of oregano, upon not overdoing it.

Jesus Christ came to a people whose lives were steeped in the law. Their every act was hedged about by rules and regulations so painfully detailed as to be understood only by full-time religious scholars. Those whom necessity forced to tasks other than the study of Torah had little hope of remaining spiritually "clean." And they tended to feel degraded by their inability to meet the requirements of ritual purity.

It was perfectly natural, then, for Jesus, and for Paul after him, to speak the language of grace in dramatic terms. To make people understand the breadth of God's love meant helping them believe in God's mercy, meant giving them a sense of freedom from the onerous burden of accumulated prerequisites. As Moses Maimonidies pointed out, a piece of paper that has been folded in one direction cannot be flattened until it has been creased in the opposite direction also.

Anyone who has ever comforted a nightmare-frightened child with the assurance that there is nothing to fear in the darkness understands the dynamics of this process. There can be much to fear in the darkness. But it is not what the child thinks it has just seen or heard.

The mercy of God makes persuasive sense only to those who fear

God's judgment. And over the centuries the repeated emphasis of Christian thought upon divine forgiveness has tended to obscure that hard reality. More and more theologians have tried to say all that must be said of God in the compassionate language of the New Testament, have tried to cram the complex majesty of the divine nature into its redemptive manifestation.

As a result the very idea of grace has become difficult to grasp, and the community of faith to which it is so relentlessly proclaimed is threatened by the loss of both vitality and form. Thus, the quite fragmentary image of the historical Jesus is offered as a full and sufficient model for piety. And human undertakings motivated by creativity and justice are in religious circles treated as somehow inferior to those prompted by compassion.

Taken as spice to the diet of biblical faith, grace adds flavor to the dish and encourages us to eat heartily and with pleasure. Taken as a meal in itself, it can become sickening!

I still believe that grace is what occurs when human penitence and divine compassion meet. Both are necessary, and to dismiss the importance of the first is to turn God into the Cosmic Slob!

Neo-Conformity

November, 1978

There is a new kind of conformity mania abroad in the land today. Something called "sensitivity." And as one who survived the furies loosed by Martin Dies, J. Parnell Thomas and Joe McCarthy, I can testify to its virulence. In our looking-glass world people are encouraged to express themselves in veritable rhapsodies of obscenity and subversion, *provided* such entertainments hurt no one's feelings. But if they do, God help you!

I first detected symptoms of the regnant tyranny in my preaching classes a few years ago. They appeared more as an absence than a presence. The absence of a vigorously critical spirit among my students as they reacted to what had been inflicted upon them by an obviously unprepared, slipshod classmate.

Sermons that would have been torn to pieces in the days when Harvey Cox wore black box toes and Bill Coffin white bucks have come more and more to be treated like something found by a shrewd Bedouin in a Dead Sea cave. They are unrolled with tender solicitude and always found to contain some amazingly subtle revelation. And the rebellious spirit who breaks the holy hush is likely to be rebuked by the reminder that "as Christians we ought to be supportive, not critical."

But the full force of the zeitgeist did not hit me until I ventured, in a sermon of my own in Battell Chapel, to offer some comments on the current state of Christian sexual morality. I did not stake out some recidivist Puritan position. But I did suggest that there are problems in the realm of human sexual behavior that cannot be solved by the simplistic aphorisms which pass for ethical norms today (e.g. "As long as we *love* one another it's O.K.").

After the service, during the coffee hour, I was told in no uncertain and barely civil terms not that I was *wrong,* but that I had been "insensitive." Did I not realize, I was asked in various ways, that there were men and women in the congregation whose bedroom behavior was called into question by my sermon? How could I have been so callous as to discuss such problems in the pulpit?

In Battell Chapel of all places! From a platform that had so lately and often rung with the most biting condemnations of presidents, generals, cabinet members and red-neck sheriffs.

During the days when such prophetic pronouncements were weekly fare no one in my hearing ever suggested that there might be in the pews the wives, siblings and children of servicemen in Viet Nam, and that *their* feelings might be wounded by condemnations of that "dirty war." And had anyone tried to moderate the passion of preaching during the civil rights struggle by urging the clergy to spare the feelings of sincere segregationists, he or she would properly have been told where to head in.

Now I am not making a case for sharp-tongued brutality in dealing with painful human problems. On the contrary, I am so weak-stomached that recent references to police officers as "pigs" disgusted me. And the attribution of endemic incest to one's political opponents makes me want to throw up. As a longtime teacher of preaching, I understand only too well that denouncing people from the pulpit is useful only for relieving the preacher's frustrations.

But as an old hand at polemical discussion, I prize highly the vigorous give and take from which some semblance of truth can begin to emerge. And I deeply resent the increasingly common effort to stifle such debate on the ground that truth may embarrass those committed to error.

There is much happening in this world that cries out for plain speaking. We ought not remain silent about the irresponsible antics of gender and ethnic chauvinists, for example, simply because they represent constituencies which have suffered much. Nor can we afford to moderate expressions of ethical rigor out of concern for the feelings of people trapped in self-destructive lifestyles. As a weapon of censorship the demand for "sensitivity" is subtle and dangerous.

Now let's have no unkind responses to this column, please. I bleed easily!

A distinguished professor of ethics was once told that a particular comment of his was "insensitive," and he replied, "Show me where the hell in the Bible it says that I must be sensitive!"

Society Has Rights, Too!

April, 1979

Two decades ago the United States went through a lively campaign to achieve the reform of its electoral districts. Under the banner "One Man (sic) One Vote," eager legions swarmed to assail the rural establishment and win for urban masses the political power to which their numbers and democratic theory entitled them. Zealous democrats had become fed up with having one legislator represent fifty thousand constituents while another spoke for half a million.

One of the most memorable slogans of this crusade was the insistence that "Trees, rocks and cows don't count. Only people do!" And if memory serves me accurately even the *New Haven Register* forsook the shade of Thomas Jefferson on the issue and supported some daringly liberal proposals. It seemed clear to all right-thinking people that basic principles were at stake in the struggle. Few responsible voices were raised in support of "rotten boroughs."

Looking back only a few years, and seeing it in the light of contemporary ecological concerns, the absolute assurance of those days that "trees, rocks and cows do not count" makes one a little uneasy. A generation that is discovering the hard way that many of earth's natural resources *are* exhaustible may be pardoned for having some reservations about the absolute disenfranchisement of Mother Nature. For whatever else must be said about the traditional favoring of rural interests in the councils of American government, it tended to protect a number of environmental values which fare rather badly in the hands of urban majorities. Rotten boroughs now seem somewhat less contrary to the will of God than they once appeared to be.

I ponder this matter whenever I see a television appeal for the conservation of natural resources. And I wonder whether we are prepared to apply the lessons learned in the past few years to another kind of vital environmental concern, the preservation of certain traditional social values which are displeasing to the current spirit of the age.

It is clear that no single human generation has a right to bankrupt the earth in pursuit of even its noblest aspirations. Nor has any single generation a right to ravage marriage, family and community, and plunder sexuality as ours is doing. The little children who look out at us from the T.V. tube reminding us that they and their peers are entitled to forests, mountains and fields may someday find their own offspring making a similarly plaintive appeal for parents, neighborhoods and even identifiable names.

The current notion that individuals and pairs have the right radically to revamp social structures and disclaim traditional responsibilities in the headlong quest for self-fulfillment is just another version of the older lie, "God sees only persons, not cities, states and nations." In that false faith, hosts of pietists marched away from their duties as Christian citizens or discharged those duties in wholly secular fashion, ostensibly to protect the purity of true religion. And they were encouraged in this retreat by those for whom one way of making conscience irrelevant is as good as any other.

Just as many kinds of assaults upon nature have irreversible consequences, some of our present-day denigration of responsible human community may lead us where no thoughtful man or woman really wants to go. Yet many of the people who are most vigilant in their protests against the pollution of nature often exhibit a sublime indifference to the gross corruption of the social order. Item: An instruction sheet mailed out to those assembling to protest the building of a nuclear power plant reminded the crusaders to provide their own contraceptive devices, since the organizing committee could not be responsible for making them available to spontaneously significant relationships!

In the sense that rocks, trees and rivers have rights, social structures have them also. For they are the means by which life is kept truly human.

If this seems a bit far-fetched, what about the current enthusiasm for animal *rights?*

Of Dentists and Divines

November, 1979

Before he became the perennial Socialist candidate for President of the United States, Norman Thomas was a Presbyterian minister. Fresh out of Union Seminary, he had an experience which helped to disenchant him with the church and figured often in his speeches questioning the effectiveness of Christian social action.

In his first job search Thomas agreed to candidate at a church located in one of New England's most notorious "company towns." He made a shrewd guess about the composition of the congregation in such a setting and prepared a fiery sermon on the need for radical reforms in American economic life. And his assumption was justified. In the front pew that Sunday sat the owner of a large and exploitive textile mill, a man who exuded authority and was deferred to in obvious ways by those around him.

Thomas was no more intimidated by the reality than he had been by the prospect and proclaimed the Word with all the forceful oratory of which he was so capable. When the service ended he took satisfaction from the realization that he had thrown away an excellent career opportunity in the service of truth!

One can imagine the young minister's amazement, then, when shortly afterward a committee of the congregation waited upon him to extend a call.

"Why, it must have taken great courage," he said, "to choose me over the objections of Mr. X."

"Well," the chairman admitted with some embarrassment, "he's the one who really wants you. He says that the pulpit is the only place for your kind of talk."

Seasoned preachers should have little difficulty identifying with what Thomas felt at that point. The clerical role does tend to disarm the prophetic arsenal. People have come to expect us to say "challenging" or even "outrageous" things. And they are very likely to be grateful for the context which puts them in italics, so that no one will confuse our words with good sense. This attitude can be very frustrating. No less effective a preacher than the late Halford Luccock once complained that congregations were dismayingly tolerant of even his most biting social criticism.

But if this role insulation causes us some concern, it also offers important compensations. It gives us a special way in which to cope with the "heartaches and the thousand natural shocks" to which flesh is heir. They become the data with which our training, temperament and vocation are supposed to equip us to deal. We often work out neat "professional" attitudes toward issues which plague the laity.

I learned this many years ago as a student at the University of Michigan when I went to the School of Dentistry for a free checkup and repair job on my teeth. (They did that sort of thing as a kind of practicum for their students.)

When I returned for my second visit, to get a report on my X-rays, I was greeted like some sort of celebrity. The teacher in charge of my file ushered me to a special room, had my arrival announced over the public address system and arranged about fifty of his apprentices according to height in a semi-circle around my chair, so they could all get a clear view of my mouth.

It turned out that I suffered from a rare kind of cyst, the treatment of which would require nerve extraction, bone scraping and root resection of four teeth. I was, in short, a highly prized opportunity for several of the students to get invaluable experience under expert supervision. And the prospective beneficiaries of my plight were more than delighted.

In some respects ministers stand in the same position vis-a-vis the men and women to whose needs they apply their vocational talents. What are for most people the bitter necessities or tragic sacrifices of life are the data with which the pastor has been called and prepared to deal. And even the grimmer aspects of such a relationship offer some psychological compensations.

One young cleric who had lost his post over protests against the Viet Nam war put it candidly when he said, "There is a certain satisfaction in this minor martyrdom. For the first time in my life I have real evidence that I have been faithful to my call. Once the shock wears off, it feels great."

The implications of all this go far beyond what it says about social action. Much of what "feels great" to preachers does so because it is their professional "thing," as well as an aspect of the faith which they share with their congregations. Those fascinating theological innovations, new ethical insights and biblical discoveries cannot be expected to strike the laity with quite the force they bring to bear upon the pulpit. For most people religious discourse is a *means* by which to understand more fully the important experiences of *their* daily lives. It is not an end in itself. And much of what excites the clergy, socially and intellectually, does so because it goes with their territory and is what they have been especially equipped to appreciate. Understanding the full implications of that fact can be the beginning of effectiveness in ministry.

I have since learned that I was one of the early guinea pigs for root canal surgery and that the professor who did the work has become known as the "grandfather" of the technique. He must have been good. I still have those teeth fifty years later!

Rape Is a Sexual Act

January, 1980

Recently in a nocturnal rendezvous with radio, I heard it said once again that "Rape is not a sexual act. It is an act of aggression." The statement was made with the kind of authority that characterizes conventional wisdom when it is expressed on talk shows. So the other members of the panel murmured agreement and quickly moved on to discuss ways and means of straightening out public opinion on the subject.

As one who shrinks from any uninvited intimacy, I have always regarded rape as an unspeakable crime and favor the death penalty for its more heinous forms. But lately I have begun to wonder about this perfervid insistence that rape is not sexual in nature, when every counsel of common sense argues that it is. And I have concluded that there are at least three reasons for our contemporary revisionism about forced carnal knowledge.

First, I suspect that some people find it more comfortable to talk about rape in terms of hostility and aggression, because they still have some hang-ups about candid discussions of sex. If we wish to mobilize public opinion behind programs to prevent "sexual assault," the whole matter can be dealt with more comfortably when emphasis is placed upon the second word in the phrase. What needs to be said about police procedures, methods of self-defense and so on goes more smoothly and with equal effectiveness when one focuses upon the violence rather than its objective.

Second, by minimizing the sexual aspects of rape we are able to camouflage our general complicity in the crime. Individuals and business enterprises feel free to maintain a constant barrage of titillation in personal demeanor, provocative clothing styles, advertising, and entertainment on the specious ground that the atmosphere of super-heated sexuality thus generated has nothing whatever to do with sexual violence. We piously put the blame upon a tired assortment of general social ills and go on merrily manipulating lust for both ego gratification and economic gain.

But there is, I am persuaded, a third reason for our reluctance to acknowledge the true character of rape, i.e. violent sex. And that is the fact that the atrocity says something disturbing about the very nature of human sexuality.

Sex obviously has a dark side, as does every other human capacity. Far from being merely the symptom of another corruption resident above the waist, sexual assault can be the motivating force behind various kinds of aggression. For human desires are not easily categorized and kept in separate compartments. They play back and forth in subtle reciprocities.

It may not be the case that cave men actually enjoyed hitting women on the head and dragging them to bed by the hair. But it is clear that primitive peoples often raided one another for no more exalted purpose than the abduction of females, not always for service in the kitchen.

Violence and sexual desire have been closely associated since the dawn of time, one encouraging the other. Immediately before and after battle both men and women engage in sexual behavior of a kind and intensity not characteristic of more tranquil periods. And there is sound reason to believe that if power is an aphrodisiac, violence is one of its distillates.

Why, then, are we so skittish about admitting the harsh fact of life? Because our age wants desperately to believe that all sex is inherently good, that any activity that is authentically *sexual* in nature ought to be encouraged or at least tolerated. It is convenient to suppose that the promptings of our glands are infallible guides to virtue and that they always conduce to significant relationships and interpersonal binding.

In this spirit promiscuity becomes "reaching out to a rich variety of others at the deepest level of need." Adultery is converted into "open marriage," something that can broaden personality. Marital covenants can be dispensed with casually in order to release the partners to fulfill their "human potential." And even the boundaries of gender become irrelevant in the search for self-expression. If it is really sexual, it must be O.K.

So it is necessary to insulate the heat of desire against cold reason. Rape is removed from the lexicon of sexual pathologies by the simple expedient of abolishing the concept of sexual pathologies. It is shifted into the category of social statement, a protest against unemployment, poor housing, imperialism or a vitamin deficiency. And we are left free to exploit our irresponsible impulses without guilt.

This one brought several letters from women thanking me for having helped in a small way to restore sanity to the discussion of rape. There were, of course, letters of a different tone, also.

Another False Dichotomy

April, 1980

The ghost of Adam Smith walks abroad in the West again today in the person of Nobel Laureate economist Milton Friedman. The honorary Dean of the "Chicago School," as the monetarist version of Manchester liberalism is called, presides over a public television series designed to reconvert America to unfettered free enterprise. It is his thesis that we shall all be better and happier people if the humanizing hand of social policy is lifted from business activities and primitive instincts are loosed to pursue their acquisitive ends with neither let nor hindrance.

Many intelligent people (including one of my sons!) find Friedman's arguments persuasive. Having discovered the delights of laissez-faire, laissez-allez in other areas of their lives, great numbers of our younger citizens are tempted to adopt it as a general principle of social disorganization.

In strictly *economic* terms what Friedman says makes a good bit of sense. People do tend to work more energetically when their labors are uninhibited by humane considerations, when the rewards for success and the penalties for failure are dramatic. And the pathetic record of Socialism in various parts of the world hardly inspires confidence. Those who try to debate the disciples of the Chicago School on purely materialistic grounds are in for a tough time.

But once again Americans are being offered, under academically respectable auspices, the great lie that the market mechanism can function effectively only when it is permitted to make all the rules of the game — and then break them when they become inconvenient. The process of allocating resources by means of the price structure, say the new Manchester liberals, must not be inhibited by social value judgments, or it will be unable to do its job.

The truth, as the distinguished anti-Socialist economist Wilhelm Roepke pointed out, is that the market economy can operate effectively within a variety of social frameworks. It is not necessary to let business shape the human image and community to its own advantage in order to reap the benefits of the price mechanism. Society can lay down some basic ground rules and insist that market forces work within them. And when this is done intelligently it need not damage the animating spirit of free enterprise.

Take an analogy from the world of sports: The fighting zeal of football teams is not destroyed by the requirement that they take only four downs to advance the ball ten yards and are not permitted to use knives or guns in the process. Having accepted the rules by which the game is defined, they may cheat from time to time, but they are not rendered listless by the limitations imposed upon them.

According to the disciples of Friedman, however, business must be allowed to turn the social order into an adjunct to its own quest for profits. Consumers must apparently be manipulated by advertising to lust after an ever-increasing variety of junk. Families, neighborhoods and whole towns must be at the disposal of "mobility." And every employer ought to be free to skim the cream from the labor market, leaving the disadvantaged and handicapped to a kind of dole or private charity.

It is a little as though the engine in your automobile were to announce that it would operate only if you travelled in a specified direction. When an economic mechanism which should be serving social values tries instead to subvert them for its own internal convenience, it reverses what Adam Smith himself regarded as the right ordering of things.

Admittedly, efforts to change the present situation would require a period of difficult adjustment. Every time the rules of an athletic contest are altered there appear diehards who announce, in effect, that without the spitball the national pastime is doomed. If the United States were to adopt the principle that competitive enterprise must work within the outlines of a humane social policy many economic superstars would sulk from the field, briefly.

In time, however, men and women adjust to new rules and begin to exert their imaginative energies within them, especially when their incomes are dependent upon their cooperation. If Detroit were told, for example, that it must produce automobiles appropriate to current needs and stop trying to tease the public into lusting after four-wheeled yachts, it would mope a bit and then turn its undoubted genius to the designated task. Provided firmly stated national policy made it clear that moping would not restore the ancien regime.

The United States does not face a stark choice between totalitarian planning and guerilla warfare capitalism. It can evolve a society in which the market mechanism works within responsible structures to achieve humane goals.

In such an undertaking the churches need to make their voices heard. For what is at stake is not only the good society, but the human self-image as well. So long as it remains profitable to stimulate lust, envy and rampant consumerism the dignity of the individual will be under insidious attack by highly sophisticated professionals.

My younger son is now an investment banker and delights in sending me newspaper clippings detailing the dismal failure of various experiments in social planning. Thank God, he is still sufficiently human about foreign policy issues to vote correctly!

Freedom Football

November, 1980

Once upon a time there was a town filled with people who loved football. On crisp Saturday afternoons in autumn everyone who was not bedridden or in jail would go to the municipal stadium to watch two local teams battle one another on a well-turfed gridiron.

Naturally the competing squads accumulated ardent fans. Men, women and children attached themselves to the Blue Team or the Red Team and backed their favorites with cheers, songs, banners, small wagers and occasional tavern brawls. A few limbs were broken, on and off the field, but such casualties were known to build a healthy competitive spirit and develop character in the young. Besides, the local veterans organization collected a small admissions charge at each game and used the money to buy every high school senior a beautiful American flag lapel pin, upon which was superimposed a flesh-toned picture of Richard Nixon and the words, "When the going gets tough the tough get going." (The Mayor's brother-in-law had quite a quantity of these adornments left over from an unfortunately timed "Support Our President" Rally which had been set to take place the day after Mr. Nixon resigned in protest against the gross ingratitude of the American public!)

One bright October afternoon, however, during the half-time festivities a very strange thing happened. A figure dressed in a clown suit ran onto the field carrying a bullhorn.

"Ladies and gentlemen," he shouted, "it seems to me that we are playing this game in a highly legalistic fashion. Our whole emphasis is upon rules and regulations rather than freedom and possibility. Why should we require one side to advance the ball exactly ten yards in order to keep possession of it? We ought to be more relaxed about the matter and let the team that appreciates it keep the ball, as long as it demonstrates a good spirit. And should it be necessary for the ball to be carried into the end zone for a score? I propose that we give points for imaginative choreography in the backfield and a cheerful demeanor in the line."

Most of the spectators were nonplussed by these proposals. But they loved football. And anything that promised to improve the game commended itself to them. They feared, also, to seem too rigid, lest their neighbors suspect them of being conservatives. So they called out approval of what the man in the clown suit suggested. Some of them even got far enough into the spirit of things to start making additional proposals of their own.

"Why are the same players on the same side throughout the game? Let's rotate the linemen after each play," cried one.

"A great idea," shouted another. "But is there any reason why only twenty-two men are having all the fun, while the rest of us just sit and watch? I say we should all get really *involved* and feel more *relevant* to the fray."

Upon hearing these words the crowd rose from its seats and clambered over the barrier onto the field. Spare balls were brought out from the locker rooms and tossed into the milling throng. A glorious melee broke out. People ran now one way and then another, helping both teams with splendid impartiality. The whole scene was one of glorious freedom and enthusiastic participation.

When the setting sun heralded the onset of evening (the time-keepers had been trampled to death by the throng) and a faint chill crept into the air, the man in the clown suit announced that the game had ended. All the people gathered in a great circle around the edges of the field, held hands and sang "Amazing Grace."

On their way home from the stadium everyone agreed that it had certainly been a wonderful afternoon and that their favorite sport had undergone a marvelous liberation. But no one ever went out to the field again. That was the last football game.

A couple of letters condemned my "attack on sports." We do our best here. But obviously a few get through half-baked.

The Peace That Passes Understanding

January, 1981

Let's state it frankly. I do not like what has happened to the "passing of the peace" in modern church services. It troubles me liturgically and psychologically. And I wish that the practice could either be reformed or abolished completely.

I realize that the peace has roots deeply planted in the ancient Christian community and is performed decently and in order in many congregations today, i.e. one person takes the hands of a neighbor between his or her own and says quietly, "The peace of Christ be with you."

But in most of the churches in which the peace is passed in our time, it has taken on the character of a dry coffee hour or a bush league orgy. Preachers descend from their pulpits to chat up the front pews. Ushers urge visitors' cards upon strangers. Old friends wisecrack about yesterday's golf games. And committee members get in a bit of discreet politicking about next month's agenda. There is much backslapping bonhomie and no little embarrassment about the whole business.

More vexatious to me personally are the most ardent forms of the rite in which people rush about the sanctuary to hug, kiss and pat bottoms like professional football players, greeting one another with an almost lascivious enthusiasm. Their faces suddenly wreathed in quite artificial smiles, men and women embrace in a manner more appropriate to *eros* than to either *agape* or *phileo.* Viewed with some detachment the proceedings remind me of nothing so much as a painting entitled "Bacchus Holds Court" which attracted my prurient attention in the public library when I was a boy.

Now some uncharitable souls will attribute my attitude to an ingrained aversion to physical contact with others. Not so! I grew up in one of the most tactile families ever to skip out of South Germany one step ahead of conscription. We hugged, kissed and patted one another to a fair-thee-well whenever two or three were gathered together in anyone's name. And woe to the unwary guest who answered carelessly when asked, "Have you had your Christmas goose yet?"

But there is an appropriate place for everything. And there is a style suited to liturgical settings which ought not be confused with more unstructured fellowship. If our churches are really communities, they will provide ample opportunities for cordial social exchanges and various personal contacts. It should not be necessary to cram them all into one superheated moment and pretend that we are groping one another for the greater glory of God.

Seriously, folks, there are at least two things wrong with the current practice.

First, it injects a note of wholly artificial fellowship into the midst of what should be a unified expression of communion with one another and with God. A well run service will bring participants into a deep awareness of their common humanity in the presence of the divine. It will generate an atmosphere of corporate involvement from beginning to end. Not by an infusion of coffee hour or a soupcon of office Christmas party, but by the quiet influence of acts performed together in prayer and praise. Much of what happens in the passing of the peace today is as inappropriate to this ethos as a formal handshake during the transports of erotic union.

Second, the present pattern is often more divisive than unifying. The traditional hand-between-hands greeting, accompanied by a simple salutation, expresses a Christian love which does not discriminate, which addresses friend and stranger in the same fashion. In contrast, the more informal practice obtaining in so many places encourages varying intensities of warmth. So that far from being welcomed by the passing of the peace many a visitor feels more excluded during this moment than at any other point in the service. The veritable explosion of *gemütlichkeit* only serves to underscore his or her strangeness and breaks rudely into the spirit engendered by the rest of the liturgy. And I can personally testify to the bruising impact of a curtly muttered "Peace!" as an indignant reader of one of these columns brushes by me in a hurry to embrace someone more worthy of blessing.

Ah, well. Perhaps I should feel differently about the whole matter, if I were not always standing next to some bearded male when the smooching starts in Marquand Chapel.

This one was reprinted in several church magazines and brought me twenty-eight letters, all but one favorable.

A Relative Matter

April, 1981

"So you teach at a divinity school," the young man said. "I used to take religion very seriously myself. Until I discovered how culturally conditioned all those biblical imperatives really are. Once you put such things in their proper context life becomes a lot more pleasant, to say the least."

"Do you really regard *all* scriptural imperatives as culturally conditioned?" I asked. "Even the Ten Commandments?"

"Oh, especially the Ten Commandments. Take that one about doing no murder. Israel, you must remember, was a very small nation surrounded by sprawling pagan populations. In a situation like that individual lives have a value which they simply cannot claim in a time such as our own, when teeming masses threaten to sink the globe under their weight. Murder has to be sternly forbidden when you are trying as a people to survive under those circumstances."

"Interesting," I murmured mendaciously. "What about 'Thou shalt not steal'?"

"*Obviously* culturally conditioned" came the reply. "The Israelites were a nomadic people. They carried all their possessions around on their own backs or on their beasts of burden. Now when you are compelled to get along on such limited supplies the theft of anything is especially painful and likely to cause serious strife in the community. You surely don't imagine, do you, that God interdicts theft in the same absolute way in a time like our own, a day of affluence in which people complain constantly about having too many *things* cluttering up their lives?"

"And adultery?" I asked.

"I hoped you would raise that one," came the triumphant response. "Everybody knows that the Jews were hung up on genealogy. They got their kicks talking about their ancestors. Remember all those 'begats' in the Bible? Israel seemed to have a morbid need to know who fathered whom. Probably something rooted in cultic superstition. But in any case when you care so much about who begat whom you view adultery with special abhorence, because it fouls up the genealogical data."

"But," he went on, "in our day we laugh at that kind of concern for family trees and poke fun at people who talk about their ancestors. So it's really silly to suppose that adultery is inherently sinful in our culture. Why, with all the kids hyphenating their names when they marry, in a couple of generations it's going to be impossible to trace anyone's lineage. So why be uptight about the sleeping arrangements?"

"Well, uh, ur," I answered incisively, "can we also relativize the commandment about bearing false witness?"

"Naturally," came the confident reply. "Israel's religion, as you know all too well, was very legalistic. Even today Jews see God as the divine Judge and his will as Law. Now in such a context bearing witness is terribly important. False witness mucks up the whole system. It has ontological significance. But we are not under the Law. We live by grace. So a little creative bending of the truth can hardly be condemned categorically, especially if it spares someone's sensitivities."

"I know it sounds stupid," I confessed, "but how about not bowing down to idols? Is that an outdated commandment?"

"In a sense it is the most archaic of them all! Think for a moment about the kinds of idols with which Moses was familiar. Moloch, Chemosh, Marduk, Baal. Nasty brutes who demanded human sacrifice, castrations and other cruel forms of worship. Naturally Israel was forbidden that sort of deity.

"But what sorts of 'idols' compete with Yahweh in the Twentieth Century? Sports heroes, financial tycoons, movie stars. Sordid, perhaps, but surely not in a class with Moloch. Did anyone ever threaten to hurl you into the fiery embrace of Marilyn Monroe?"

"No," I whined piteously.

"Well, there you are."

At this point the train slowed for the Westport station and my seatmate rose to leave.

"I hope we run into one another again," he said. "I'd like to share some of my insights into the First Chapter of Romans. They'd probably surprise you."

"Don't bet on it." I muttered at his retreating back. "Don't bet on it."

One student asked quite seriously whether I had actually had this conversation. He is now a bishop in a church which shall be nameless.

A Modest Proposal to the Moral Majority

November, 1981

To hear people talk about the deceitfulness of politicians one might suppose that the mendacity of public officials represents some grotesque departure from an American norm. Having observed politics closely for years I am under no illusions about the devotion of its practitioners to the truth. When it serves their purposes those who govern us are quite willing to tailor facts artfully. And those who *seek* to govern us usually outdo those in power in imaginative adjustments of historical data.

But in such self-serving creativity the public sector cannot hold a candle to the private sector. American business has raised deception to new levels of effectiveness and has invented kinds of double-talk that must have Tallyrand breaking all records for subterranean r.p.m.

Indeed, it is not unfair to suggest that misrepresentation is a basic dynamic of our national economy. It helps keep the wheels of industry turning. And there is some reason to believe that a sudden conversion to truth-telling might produce a cataclysmic depression in the United States.

Think for a moment of how many jobs depend upon gulling the public. If people ever faced the fact that there is virtually no difference among beers and cigarettes or that many of the packaged products sold in grocery supermarkets are interchangeable in all important respects, many producers and wholesalers would go to the wall overnight.

The American consumer supports hordes of unnecessary jobs and acres of duplicated plant equipment because he or she is misled into supposing that they are necessary to a vital freedom of choice among significantly diverse products.

And why does this misunderstanding arise? Turn on your television set any evening of the week, and the answer leaps out at you with all the violence of a cop show and the seductive subtlety of a risque situation comedy. Some of this nation's best brains and most creative imaginations spend their well-rewarded lives generating a demand for totally unnecessary gadgets, exorbitantly priced status symbols and useless lotions. The business of fabricating urgent needs from the whole cloth is both big and profitable today.

The economic implications of this charlatanism are horrendous. If the wealth that is poured into worthless products, their packages and the fabulously expensive campaigns by which they are made to seem important were turned to meeting real human needs, many of the world's most serious problems would begin to move toward solutions. No Christian can look at the pinched faces, bloated bellies and fly-blown sores of African and Asian children or confront the indignity visited by poverty upon countless of his or her own neighbors without being sickened by the way the earth's resources, human and material, are squandered on behalf of artificially created appetites.

But the economic waste is only half the story. Think what happens to the hearts and minds of the men and women who spend their lives and talents engaged in the practice of deliberate and artful deception. What must it be like to go off to work every morning knowing that you will be using the great gifts of intelligence and imagination to exploit your neighbors and millions of people all over the world? What does it do to the human psyche to be publicly applauded at elaborate award ceremonies for having come up with the most effectively persuasive bit of deception in packaging or sales promotion?

Many years ago the now defunct magazine, *The Reporter,* printed an article describing the brain drain from education, social services and psychotherapy into the posh offices of motivation research firms on Madison Avenue. Every year some of the top graduates of behavioral science programs in our greatest universities hire themselves out to organizations which specialize in misleading the public. With what cost to human values only God knows.

If the Moral Majority really wants to expose corruption and sin in American life, it need not concentrate on pornographic movies and abortion clinics. There is an abundant supply of it available in a society which uses the ferment of moral decay as leaven.

One of our graduates who has abandoned the pulpit in favor of public relations work in New York assured me that this column revealed obvious "Communist sympathies."

A Very Present Help

April, 1982

A character in one of C.P. Snow's novels gives a friend this bit of advice about politics. "The secret of success," he says, "can be stated in two words, 'Be there!'"

It took me a long time to learn that lesson. For years I assumed that in democratic institutions policy decisions are made in formal convocations to which all concerned people are summoned for the purpose of shaping the common future. Oh, I understood that things went on in lobbies and cloakrooms and that perfervid speeches accomplished less than I might have wished. But the tremendous importance of just *being there* had to be learned the hard way.

During my first years on the New Haven Board of Aldermen I was troubled by a vague sense of what might be called "premature closure." That is, time and time again issues in which I had a keen interest, issues that I had looked forward to debating on the floor of the chamber, had for all practical purposes been settled before the body ever convened. And our public meetings often turned out to be fairly pro forma.

At first I tended to view this as some sort of nefarious conspiracy. The bosses, I concluded, were pulling the strings and making the rest of us dance to their tune. And there was an element of justification to that suspicion. But with the passage of time and experience I came to realize that as often as not our prearranged decisions reflected not a command but a consensus, a consensus that had developed in the course of those unofficial contacts that the Aldermen had with one another in the course of their daily lives. And knowing this is an important part of understanding democracy.

The local grocery store manager and filling station operator, for example, are likely to have a good bit of influence on community affairs. Not because they can cut off people's supplies of food and gasoline, but because the nature of their jobs makes it possible, indeed necessary, for them to be in daily touch with the public attitudes and to shape them in subtle ways.

Lawyers spend a fair amount of time waiting in corridors outside courtrooms. Their conversation very often turns to political developments in which they have an interest. And deals get struck quite spontaneously. Men and women who belong to the same churches, lodges and ethnic societies transact, often unwittingly, a lot of public business in those contexts. Unlike European political parties which hold annual policy conferences, American politics is frequently done in settings which reflect other purposes and interests.

One may want to deplore that fact and try to limit its impact, for its dangers are obvious. But realism requires us to acknowledge that the formation of consensus in any kind of community does not depend entirely upon formal meetings called for an announced purpose. Much of it occurs wherever two or three are gathered for fun or profit. One who wants to be heard had better plan to "be there."

This does not mean that individuals must don disguises and sneak under the tentflaps into gatherings to which they are not in normal course invited. It does imply, however, a responsibility to be sufficiently involved in the *total life of the community* to be aware of what is happening and to be able to influence events in the early stages of their formation. Those who wait around for engraved invitations to conventicles at which *Issues Touching Upon the Destiny of the Human Race* are to be resolved will wait in vain.

What holds true in public politics also obtains in the affairs of various social institutions. I recently finished a novel in which a woman professor at Harvard is depicted as suffering from a sense of isolation and irrelevance in that setting. She attributes this to her gender and the age-old prejudices of her male colleagues. But the novelist, a feminist herself, soon makes it clear that her protagonist dislikes cocktail and dinner parties, abhors faculty luncheons, cannot stand the tedium of the master's common room and will, in fact, gather only with a few intimates over white wine and the "Goldberg Variations."

Whatever *ought* to be the case, people talk about their primary interests in other than official boardrooms. They discuss what is on their minds and often reach preliminary conclusions about these matters in the interstices of daily life. And when they gather to weigh issues in formal convocation those casual conversations cannot be expunged from their memories.

So those who elect to spend their time in limited associations within intellectual, confessional, ethnic or gender enclaves ought not be surprised when their influence upon events is less than they might like it to be.

I am persuaded that what is called the "Establishment" in any given social organization consists largely of those who have had the good sense, commitment and self-discipline to "be there."

I have become inceasingly persuaded that this is one of the best bits of advice that can be given to women, minority groups and others excluded from the social decision making process. Always "be there," and on time!

Mea (sorta) Culpa

January, 1983

Some faithful and friendly readers of these columns have written recently to express mild concern about what they regard as the increasingly conservative tone of my opinions. This does not throw me into a state of shock, because such missives have over the years been matched in both number and vehemence by correspondents who profess to see this page as a part of The International Communist Conspiracy.

A decent respect for the judgment of my peers suggests, however, that I take note of the first charge in some explicit fashion. So let me enter a plea of nolo contendere-with-extenuating-circumstances.

Many influences have combined to moderate somewhat the oracular assurance of my youthful liberalism. Some are quite commonplace, e.g. the aging process which slows down the glands and tends to stifle enthusiasm for relentless change. Or those repeated disenchantments that we call "experience." The brightest and best idols of my past, in whose van I was proud to march against unnumbered foes have turned out too often to have been grievously wrong. (Norman Thomas's insistence that World War II was just another imperialist squabble in the worst European tradition is hard to swallow while you are looking at photographs of Auschwitz and Treblinka.)

More important than these, however, has been my progressive unhappiness with liberalism's *means* orientation, its frequent assumption that the means justify the end. Some of the causes to which I subscribed years ago turn out in retrospect to have been strategies for reaching ill-defined goals rather than significant goals in themselves. And some degree of maturity forces us to understand that while journeys can be exciting adventures, their final validation lies in the destinations to which they take us. Once mere movement becomes its own reason for being it ceases even to entertain.

It is a bitter thing to discover, for example, that the fight to have James Joyce's *Ulysses* admitted to the United States and *Lady Chatterley's Lover* left intact on library shelves has dead-ended in *Deep Throat* and live sex in Times Square. Just as it cannot help distressing one to find that the Union Shop, that laudable goal of Christian social action, has been widely used to keep minority members out of the more lucrative trades.

In their zeal for an elusive thing called "progress" liberals have tended to ignore objectives and judge the fidelity of their peers by the latter's willingness to do the same.

I confess with some embarrassment that I first began to discern this mistake through the discourtesy of an emerging conservative intelligentsia. Let me explain.

During my formative years all the exciting political thought seemed to be coming from the Left. Conservatives contented themselves with their entrenched power in Coolidge-Hoover America. They felt little need to make their case in terms that might appeal to growing minds. Indeed, the intellectual was suspect among them simply by virtue of *being* an intellectual.

Again and again in my college days honest efforts to get a Republican to take part in a public debate with other points on the political spectrum were unavailing. And when an articulate member of the Right could be found he (sic) usually wrapped himself in the flag, passed on the latest rumors about President

Roosevelt's mental health and hinted darkly at Communist conspiracies in Washington. One had to be retarded or possessed of preternatural faith to take the conservative option seriously under the circumstances.

That situation has changed dramatically in recent years. A well-established liberalism has begun to reiterate worn-out nostrums with tiresome regularity, taking their credibility for granted. And a crop of disturbingly provocative intellectuals has begun to flower on the Right. They are asking questions about the relationship between ends and means which stereotypical liberalism has ruled out of court. And one can learn from them. Things that stretch and deepen the mind.

The spectrum of such commentators from Robert Nisbet and George Will through Midge Decter and Irving Kristol to Ben Wattenberg is not one on which I feel comfortable. And that is precisely why I like to visit there from time to time. These people can be taken seriously without loss of face. They *must* be taken seriously. For in responsible dialogue with their kind a tired liberalism can find new freshness and a more creative confidence in its own principles.

I still vote the straight Democratic ticket and probably always will. But, Oh Lord, how I miss Hubert Humphrey!

November 9, 1988, Oh boy, do I really miss Hubert Humphrey!

What's In A Name?

April, 1983

At the end of a three day college forensics tournament, during which my partner and I had debated eight times, a judge who had heard us in half of those contests offered a comment: "This is the perfectly balanced team. Huston has a mind like a rapier. He cuts the opposition into small pieces, holds each one up for the inspection of the audience, then tosses it aside disdainfully. Muehl has a mind like a bludgeon. He clubs his opponent's case into an unrecognizable pulp and hurls the bloody corpse at your feet."

Well, if you think you have had that bit of self-disclosure without cost, you are sadly mistaken. Having purged myself by honest confession of co-conspiracy I mean to mount an attack on that increasingly popular phenomenon, the rhetorical bludgeon.

Back in the thirties people who opposed that federation of social programs, the New Deal, often declared indignantly that it was leading the United States down the road to "Socialism." Then in the forties and fifties politicians who were bewildered by the decline in American world power were heard to blame our national reverses upon "Communism" in the State Department.

Thoughtful men and women, especially clerics and academics, were appalled by such irresponsible charges. Public policies, they argued, should be discussed in more reasonable terms, not simply stigmatized in wholesale fashion. (All of which did not prevent them from inventing the word "McCarthyism" with which to strike back at their tormentors.)

Now there are obviously times for grouping data and giving the congeries an appropriate title with which to facilitate discourse. The word "Socialism" has a proper use, i.e. to refer to a particular political program. And it is undeniably convenient to be able to refer to such a program by the use of a label rather than by reiterating its component features during every discussion of world affairs. But to hurl such words at one's adversaries because they agree at one or more points with the views summed up in such a label is cynicism of the most irresponsible kind.

Unfortunately, however, the very groups of people who would once have condemned such a practice are today prominent among its devotees. It is not at all uncommon to hear a preacher, for example, sum up the sins of the world by listing such things as "racism," "sexism," "classism," and more recently and absurdly "handicapism." Often one or more of these labels will animate the peroration of a sermon the way drinking, dancing, smoking and gambling might have done decades ago.

Used in such a manner words lose their meanings. They become merely clubs with which to beat an opponent into an "unrecognizable pulp." The tag "racism," for instance, is commonly employed today to condemn everything from white-hooded violence, on the one hand, to thoughtful reservations about the effectiveness of a particular *technique* of affirmative action on the other. And in like manner many polemicists make no distinction in their use of the word "sexism" between attitudes which would reduce all women to serfdom and that ingrained impulse (learned from their mothers) which prompts elderly gentlemen to rise when a woman enters the room.

As I have admitted, I understand all too well from personal experience the temptation which the availability of such semantic battering rams sets before the purveyor of words. How useful it is to have at hand a label which constitutes an indictment so intimidating that no bill of particulars is required or permitted! Once a word has been used for a while to refer to some substantive human depravity it can become the means of silencing those whose only crime is some difference of opinion with the speaker's or writer's point of view.

Both the users and the victims of these devices suffer. But what suffers most is rational discourse. People who rely on verbal bludgeons eventually lose their analytical edge and become more and more tempted to denounce rather than discuss. And the tone of community discourse goes into a downward spiral.

So let's have no more of this rhetorical hooliganism!

I am probably still traumatized by the time a publication of the Young Communist League referred to me as "A Social-Fascist Under Trotskyite Influence."

Bye, Bye, Rabboni

January, 1984

"And Jesus said, 'Neither do I condemn you; go, and do not sin again.'"

The woman rose from her frightened crouch and started to scurry away. But then, as though suddenly aware of Jesus' closing injunction, she stopped and looked quizzically at her rescuer.

"What do you mean, 'do not *sin* again?'" she asked.

"I think you know what I mean," Jesus replied.

"But I don't know, Rabbi, unless you are suggesting that my relationship with Reuben is *sinful*."

"What would you call it?"

"A significant relationship," the woman answered, "an interpersonal commitment in which each of us seeks to realize a full potential."

"Say what?" Jesus asked.

"Reuben and I *love* one another. Surely you know what that means. How can a relationship be sinful when it expresses love? I understand that you talk a lot about love."

"Uh, but what about your covenant with your husband?"

"Isaac? Well, Rabbi, Isaac and I have never really turned one another on. We cannot realize our full sexuality together."

"What does that have to do with . . . ?"

"O, come now, Rabboni, people have a duty to themselves, you know, a right to their happiness."

"They do?"

"Certainly. And why should we let an outmoded legalism tie us into relationships that are sterile and unfulfilling?"

Jesus appeared somewhat relieved.

"You mean that Isaac is unable to father children, and you hope that Reuben . . . ?"

"Rabbi, you're putting me on. You know very well what I mean. God knows, Isaac can father children. I have five of them to prove that."

"You have five children, and you propose to ignore your marriage vows and carry on with this man Reuben?"

"O, Rabboni, you're really cute! 'Carry on with this man Reuben.' That kind of talk went out with the Judges. I'm not saying that Reuben and I will stay together forever. We may very well outgrow one another in time and need new room to explore our authentic selfhood. People do change, you know."

"But the children?"

"Kids aren't as fragile as you think, Rabboni. You'd be surprised at how well they get along with Reuben, the way they hang on him when he stays over for breakfast. When Isaac is away on a camel drive, that is. They call him 'Uncle Rube,' and he does magic tricks for them and like that. They much prefer him to Nathan."

"Nathan?"

"My previous significant other. He got to be a terrible drag. Said his conscience bothered him and legalistic stuff like that. I told him he should pay more attention to *your* teachings."

"How might I have helped him?"

"Well, you know! Those things you say about not being paralyzed by guilt and fearing human opinion. What about your teaching that adulteresses will get into Heaven ahead of the Pharisees?"

"Ah, yes. But tell me, if this Reuben loves you so much, why wasn't he here today, when you surely needed him?"

"He wanted to be, Rabboni. He really did, very much. But he just can't stand the sight of blood. He's a very sensitive person. Not at all like Joshua."

"Joshua? Another significant . . . ?"

"O, that was over long ago. And it wasn't really significant. Not really. You might say I was just trying my wings."

"And then again I might not."

"Mmmmmm?"

"What will you say to your husband about today?"

"I'll tell him to view it as a learning experience, a chance to broaden his horizons. — Well, I must run now. Bye, bye, Rabboni. Have a good day."

Jesus gazed reflectively after the departing figure. Then he stooped once more to the ground, stretched forth his hand — and picked up a large stone.

Whew! This one really put the cat among the pigeons. And vice versa!

Matthew XXV, 31-46

April, 1984

At 2:00 a.m. on January 1, 1984, a young man named Sam Todd left a New Year's Eve party in Manhattan to get a bit of fresh air. A slender 24-year old, Sam is no stranger to the streets of New York. And standing an athletic 5'11" he has always felt able to take care of himself, especially in neighborhoods familiar to him.

Others at the party, among them his brother, offered to accompany Todd, but he politely brushed aside company and set off jogging in the vicinity of Mulberry and Huston Streets. He has not been seen since.

Sam differs in various ways from the many people who disappear in New York City every year. Among these is the fact that he is a third year student at the Yale Divinity School.

When word of their friend's absence reached the student body at Sterling Quadrangle, the response was immediate and dramatic. First by twos and threes in private cars, and then by the score in chartered buses, young men and women descended on New York and its environs in search of their fellow student.

At the outset the project was more earnest than organized. But it very quickly became both intense and carefully structured. Leaflets containing descriptions and pictures of Sam were distributed throughout the area involved and even in the suburbs. Soup kitchens, flophouses, city shelters and all other places that a missing person might turn up were visited daily. And every effort was made to coordinate the work of the amateur teams with the professional agencies of the city.

It takes neither great imagination nor knowledge of New York City to realize that for many divinity students this undertaking involved repeated contacts with kinds of people and places they had never experienced before and brashness in confronting total strangers in an impersonal city to press their inquiries.

One of the more intriguing results of this campaign was its effect upon New York police officers. They said repeatedly that they had never seen such an outpouring of effort on behalf of any missing person and acknowledged that their own efforts could not help being intensified by the cooperation being given them.

One veteran member of the force told a student that he had heard of "the ties that bind," but had never seen them before. Another commented that the phrase "Christian community" was taking on new meaning for him.

In their turn, students were deeply impressed by the attitude and zeal of the metropolitan authorities in charge of the search. In fact, some police officers seemed consciously to want to "minister" to Sam's family and friends. (One of them said, "You know, there is Someone who always knows where Sam is!") And when a telephone caller asked to speak to the person in charge of the search for Sam Todd the desk man replied, "We're all searching for Sam Todd."

At this writing Sam is still missing, and the search has become increasingly the province of professionals. The school remembers him regularly in its prayers, however, and those prayers take on depth and strength because of the action with which they have been linked.

When I first came to the Divinity School four decades ago, I was not sure that I wanted a career in theological education.

But I quickly learned that the people that I met here were the kind with whom I wanted to live and work. Experiences like the search for Sam Todd repeatedly assure me that my original decision was right. For all of our differences and tensions, there is at the heart of this community a kind of love which springs into sacrificial action when the right call is sounded.

The Grace of a Great Joy
November, 1984

Back in the late-fifties my wife and I bought a Cheverolet Corvette. We had not intended to do so when we entered the dealer's showroom that afternoon. Our minds were set on a gray station-wagon, something that would accommodate our growing family and fit into plans for cross-country camping trips.

But when the deal was almost complete, and the salesman was writing up the order, I strolled into the next room and saw there the fulfillment of every Detroit boy's dream. A fire-engine red, low-slung convertible bomb! It stood there in the neon sunlight like a glimpse of Grenada.

The price was outrageous ($4,400), and it was utterly impractical from every point of view. But my wife had recently come into a modest legacy. So, bless her heart, she said, "Let's buy it." — And we did.

For a time I was in a state of bliss. When I went off to some prep school or college to speak, young people would gather around this then-rare vehicle in awe and admiration. And the discovery that it belonged to "the preacher" shook up some quite outdated ideas about religion.

But there was one large fly in the ointment of my delight. My conscience. The knowledge of what I had spent on this luxury item haunted the fringes of my happiness and kept me in a state of guilty self-examination. How many Indian children could be fed for how long on what I had invested in that Corvette? Did I have a right to cram my family into our aging and undependable old Ford sedan in order to indulge my adolescent love affair with the automobile?

Then one weekend while I was attending a conference of secondary school chaplains in up-state New York, I spoke of these misgivings with some of the young clergy gathered in an admiring circle around my car. "I really love the thing," I confessed, "but it does seem an inexcusable extravagance, considering the other things that might be done with the money it represents."

There were murmurs of mingled dissent and agreement. And my anxiety level began to mount. Then one young Episcopal priest asked, "Muehl, have you never heard of the grace of great joy?"

No, I admitted, the phrase was unfamiliar to me.

"Well," the chaplain said, "allowing yourself some harmless but cherished fulfillment can be a form of grace. It can give a lift to your spirit and add zest to your life. It can make you more able and willing to face the sacrifices that God may ask of you in other ways. Sure, the money that it represents might be used to feed the poor and heal the sick. But the same thing can be said of the house you live in and that beautiful quadrangle in which you teach. Stop tormenting yourself and accept the grace of this great joy."

Well, that was one of the most comforting words I have ever heard. It let me see my toy in a new way and scattered the clouds of conscience that had been hanging over my spirit. I began enjoying the Corvette with unalloyed enthusiasm. And I shall always remember that homeward drive through the autumnal Cherry Valley with the top down and the hills flattening out under the two hundred and fifty horsepower!

Oh, I realized that my friend's counsel could easily become

the excuse for gross self-indulgence. But it did make a lot of sense. Joy can be a leaven for the soul. And mortal creatures from Detroit will find joy in experiences which do not follow the examples of saints. I felt certain that Martin Luther would approve.

So I delighted greatly in my red Corvette convertible — until the day I sold it a short time later and bought a station wagon.

Don't ask me to explain what happened. I guess that having been set free to enjoy my car I was set free to give it up. When the pangs of scrupulosity were stilled I was able to hear the voice of prudence and be pursuaded by it.

So here, gentle reader, is the moral of my tale: Beware of grace bearing gifts.

One reader wrote to scold me for talking about owning a Corvette when there are starving children in Africa. Am I missing something here? Or was he?

Suffer Not *the Little Children*

January, 1985

I am devoted to children. My regard for them is so great that I have been known to claim that they are the primary purpose of human sexuality, never mind all this business about tie-binding. This annoys many of my friends. Especially those who have chosen to forego parenthood in the interests of their "personal growth" or professional careers.

But I have the gravest of reservations about the presence of kids in a Sunday morning church service. And it troubles me deeply when some squirming youngster or crying infant intrudes upon the atmosphere appropriate to hearing a sermon or engaging in worship. This attitude of mine also annoys many of my friends. Especially those who feel that togetherness in the pews strengthens family life and builds good habits in the young.

Let me state my reasons for feeling as I do, as calmly as possible.

First, requiring one's offspring to sit through a church service intended for adults virtually guarantees that their first impression of religion will be one of ineffable boredom. They are very likely to take from the experience nothing so much as a determination to escape from church as soon as the law allows.

My father, scion of a devout Presbyterian family, was taken to divine worship three times every week by God-fearing parents. The day he got his first paycheck he swore off church-going and never entered the house of prayer again, except when his two sons were being married. His story is a common one these days.

Second, encouraging the distracting presence of the very young gives the wrong kind of message to their parents. It says, in effect, that the *substance* of what occurs during worship is relatively unimportant, that what really matters is the socializing experience.

Unfortunately, modern Americans are all too ready to believe this. Sermons which require thought and liturgies which assume genuine congregational participation tend to get short shrift from most of the laity. What thay want are brief pep talks and someone else doing the prayers.

Remember how often you have heard men and women say, "I get more out of the children's sermons than I do from the rest of the service." That may be a well-deserved comment on the quality of the pastor's homilies, suggesting that they are murky expositions of texts which intrigue no one.

But such remarks *can be* an indirect way of saying that religion has no relevance to the adult world, that mature men and women cannot be expected to pay attention to anything which is not stated in words of one syllable and illustrated with puppets!

We do not take the whole family to the opera, to public lectures on serious subjects or to exhibits at the modern art gallery. We understand very well that such events will bore the kids. And we are properly sensitive to the right of others to enjoy those experiences without the intrusion of childish restlessness.

I think I understand the view of those who hold otherwise. And where no adequate provision is made for the care of children during worship church members have to expect what they get. But on principle adults have rights as well as responsibilities vis-a-vis the little ones. And one of these is the right to take public worship seriously.

What about the words of Jesus on the subject? Well, handle

those the way you do the one's about taking no thought for the morrow!

Ok, so I'm getting old. But so are most of the rest of the people in the congregation. If members of Congress jump when we speak, the clergy had better pay attention!

Speak Up, For God's Sake!

April, 1985

When my late colleague Liston Pope was pastor of a small rural church in North Carolina he made a practice of calling upon members of his Sunday evening congregations to offer free prayer as a part of the service. The quality of these offerings was understandably a bit spotty. Some of the efforts smacked more of sermonettes or bills of indictment than worship. And a few were so protracted as to cause restiveness in the pews, not to mention the pulpit.

Then one night the pastor summoned an elderly senior deacon to lead the assembled throng in prayer. The old fellow got up with obvious reluctance, cleared his throat loudly and stood silently in place. Finally, at the end of a bad three minutes by the cleric's watch, Christ's elder statesman sighed audibly and said, "I don't guess I'll mess with it." — and sat down.

I think of that incident often these days when one is likely to encounter opportunities for free prayer of sorts in even mainline urban churches. More and more often clergy anywhere to the left of the late Cardinal Ottaviani are making space in their liturgies for more or less spontaneous lay participation in intercessions and thanksgivings.

In principle I approve heartily of the practice. But I do wish that those who avail themselves of the privilege would speak up loudly and clearly enough to be *heard* by those who are being asked to second their petitions. As often as not the minister's invitation is followed by a series of embarrassed or truculent mutters, audible only to those most immediately in the vicinity of the speaker. And this troubles me.

First, because I like to know what I am praying for or against. My funds on deposit with the throne of grace are very limited, to say the least. And I hate to contemplate the possibility of wasting any capital. As things now stand I live in constant fear that some Republican may have sneaked into Marquand Chapel, for example, and I shall find out too late that I have supported an appeal on behalf of Edwin Meese or preemptive strikes against the New Hebrides!

Second, it smacks of the worst legalism to suppose that prayers in support of only God-knows-what can be truly efficacious. Responding, "Lord, hear our prayer," to just any incoherent moan from the back pew is in my mind meaningless. It suggests that Christian prayer is like those prayer wheels which certain Eastern religious put in streams, so that as they turn, prayers inscribed upon them are spewed out automatically over and over again.

When Leslie Weatherhead gave his Beecher Lectures at Yale on the ministry of healing, he offered what was for me a provocative idea about intercessory prayer. Why, he asked, must we suppose that such petitions consist of tossing a bundle of concern up to God with the request that God "please bung it down on Smith or the United Nations?" Is it not possible, he continued, that the Most High has built into creation the ability of one human being to act directly upon others by prayer?

I am not quite ready to buy the whole package. But Weatherhead's suggestion does have merit. For one thing, it eliminates the idea that humanity must assault an indifferent or careless deity with requests for loving attentions which would not otherwise occur to the latter. I like the idea of getting rid of the

Reluctant Eccentric in the Sky who will help people only if others ask often enough. And intercessions viewed in this way would surely encourage greater concern than is now shown for the conscious engagement of the whole congregation in the process.

But whatever the reason, people will have to speak up clearly, if they want my support for their free prayers. I refuse to run the risk of conniving unwittingly in the perpetuation of Reaganomics!

I must confess that some of the bidding of prayers strikes me as a subtle kind of more-concerned-about-others-than-thou upmanship. People occasionally seem to vie with one another to come up with neglected causes. I have been tempted to ask intercession for any and every form of life which may exist on other planets.

"A Man Who . . ."

November, 1985

A Spaniard might say that there is "salt" in the New Haven air these days. Not the rancid smell from the harbor, but the tang of an impending municipal election. Candidates for the two major parties criss-cross the city in their quest for votes. And their war cries and mating calls "ring from all the trees," as the song says.

I inevitably view this whole process with a somewhat jaundiced eye and resurgent memories of my days of glory on the Board of Aldermen. It does seem to me that the young people in whom we now repose our hopes lack something of the character that my own nobility of spirit demonstrated in the fall of '63. Firmly I stood against all corruption. And I waged a campaign that is still talked about when the veterans of that time gather to swap lies.

You see, I did not know that I had been nominated to lose. My opponent in the Eighteenth Ward was a highly qualified and personally attractive young fellow with whom the G.O.P. maintained a visible presence in city government. My party leaders wanted to pit against him a genteel candidate. One who would lose with dignity and at the same time prove conclusively that Yale professors just do not understand politics. (A canard given the lie by every tenure review committee on which I have ever served!)

My unexpected win created something of a problem for the Town Chairman. For it gave the Democratic Party total control of all branches of municipal government, thus destroying its his-

139

toric good excuse for nonfeasance in office. ("Those obstructionist Republicans!")

Two people were responsible for the upset in the Eighteenth Ward. My wife and an amiable Texan, Homer Henderson. Ruth proved to have organizing skills never before employed. And Homer was living proof that LBJ was not unique.

Between the two Muehls we managed to call on every voter in our neighborhoods and then write them a letter of thanks for letting us in the front door. All those with any resemblance to a Yale connection had at least one arm twisted by colleagues in their departments. It would have been appalling, except for the ideal outcome which it was intended to achieve.

One day at the height of the campaign a well-meaning friend remarked that Ruth was certainly being "a devoted wife." To which that lady replied, "Devoted wife, Hell! I'm just a rotten loser."

At one point in the campaign my talent for mimicry almost got me into trouble with an influential fraction of my constituents. Visiting the Irish neighborhood I became so enchanted by its rich potpourri of accents that I began unconsciously to imitate them. Fortunately, the party worker accompanying me tipped me off just in time.

But it was in that same Irish neighborhood that I had my only real contact with a voter who was less than courteous to me. Mr. Sean Mulcahy lived on the second floor of a two-family house. When I rang his bell he came out on the upstairs porch and inquired about my business. When I explained my call he said, "Oi'm not goin' to vote this year. The party has forgotten who put it into office in the first place. And that makes me mad!"

I tried several soft answers without turning aside his wrath. So I finally lost my cool and said angrily, "Well, if you're too mad to vote Democratic, why not vote Republican?"

The retort came quickly from that second floor porch. "Oi said Oi was mad! Not crazy!"

Well, Mr. Mulcahy did turn out on election day, clad in his "funeral suit" in recognition of the seriousness of the occasion. And when he reached the polling place he . . . but that's another story and must be saved for a future date.

This kind of experience made ward politics challenging.

Keep Your Sunglasses Handy

January, 1986

My little brother had a trick that he liked to play on the rest of the family when we were out riding in the car on a sunny afternoon. He would squint ferociously and say "Gee, the glare on the road is hurting my eyes. Doesn't it bother the rest of you?"

Well, almost invariably the eyes of everyone in the car would start to burn and tear. Those who until that moment had been perfectly comfortable began to find the light reflected from the road intolerably brilliant. Even after we had caught on to my sibling's trick we sometimes reacted like Pavlov's dogs to his mischief.

As annoying as they were at the time, those occasions taught me two important lessons somewhat earlier than I might otherwise have learned them.

First, human beings will often put up with some potential or present affliction until it is called to their attention. And then they will find it insupportable.

I was reminded of this lesson many times during the most militant days of labor union organization in the thirties. One of the most difficult hurdles that union organizers had to get over was the average working stiff's patience under wages, hours and working conditions which should have stirred him or her to righteous indignation. Like preachers who have to persuade people that they are alienated and anxious, so that the gospel can be proclaimed, labor leaders were often compelled to point out the obvious repeatedly in order to win support from lethargic workers. There was, I fear, a kind of truth to the Chamber of Commerce's repeated assertions that things had been going swimmingly in such-and-such an industry, until "outside agitators" came on the scene. Consciousness raising is not as new a phenomenon as many suppose.

The second thing I was taught by my brother's prank is that even intelligent men and women can be made sensitive to afflictions that exist largely in some demagogue's game plan.

As a student at the University of Michigan during what were known as the "Popular Front" days I sometimes found myself trying to cooperate in a political venture with leaders of the Young Communist League. (They were *real* Commies, not just members of the Methodist Social Action Committee!)

One who is not blinded by intellectual openness very quickly discovered that the Young Communists were not interested in solving particular problems on campus. They wanted simply to use those problems to stir up unrest and prepare the ground for their own recruiting drives. Often, as in Germany's Weimar Republic, the comrades would cynically frustrate reforms which threatened to reduce community tensions.

In my own association with labor unions, as both teacher and arbitrator, I saw modified versions of this practice at work within them. Dissident elements in union locals were known to encourage wholly unreasonable expectations in order to put established leaders on the spot and replace them with their own candidates. Organizers for competing national unions sometimes exacerbated grievances among workers in order to persuade these latter to switch to their jurisdictions.

Every dynamic social movement is in danger of falling victim to this kind of opportunism. Responsible civil rights campaign leaders complained on occasion that even their highest achievements were denigrated by young militants who were out to build their own power bases. And more recently the efforts of women to organize more effectively have sometimes been sabotaged by those who measure the success of any movement by the degree of friction that it generates.

People who have no patience with the idea of inherent human sinfulness will tend to dismiss any discussion of such phenomena as some sort of recidivism. But those who have come to terms with the hard fact of endemic human corruption should have no difficulty understanding the pervasiveness of this risk.

Sometimes that glare on the road ahead is simply the reflection of a self-serving imagination!

This dates back to the days when the journey from Detroit to Mackinac Island took three days in a Dodge touring car, with the luggage stowed on something called the "running board."

An Election Day Denouement

April, 1986

Now, let's see, where were we? Ah, yes. Sean Mulcahy and I were having a confrontation on his front porch. He had said he was not going to vote, because he was mad at the Democrats, but would have to be crazy to vote Republican. So he planned to "sit this one out."

Well, I blew my cool at that point. And at the top of my voice I informed him that I did not want his vote! "You Irishmen," I shouted, "are always talking about your dedication to democracy and telling us how the English have trampled your rights. And now you're going to skip this election in a fit of pique. We're better off without you."

So saying, I trampled off down the street, while heads peered from behind all the lace curtains on the block. This had sounded like too good a scrap to miss, I guess. And I began to fear that I had lost more than one vote that afternoon.

Election Day dawned bright and clear. And I took up my beat in front of the polling place, where all good candidates for the Board of Aldermen spend the hours between six a.m. and eight p.m. I was ready for a day of handshaking and smiling, while my confederates ran the headquarters and drove people to the voting booths.

Mid-morning I received a note from the Ward Chairman telling me to go over to Winchester Avenue and pick up a Mr. Mulcahy for a ride to the polling place. This was quite a departure from

145

the usual procedure. And I wondered how many of my potential voters would use my absence as an excuse for voting Socialist.

I parked in front of Mr. Mulcahy's house, and he came out in his funeral suit, carrying his blackthorne stick. I tried to greet him warmly as though our earlier contretemps had not happened. But he spoke not a word. All the way to the firehouse he kept a stony silence, as I chatted sweatily in an affort to establish some rapport.

My passenger got out at the polls and marched in to exercise his inalienable right. He returned so quickly that it was obvious that he had pulled only the party lever. And I could not help wondering whether he had ceased to be "mad" or had simply gone "crazy."

Back to Winchester Avenue we went. Since it was too late to change anything by my charm, I rode as silently as old Sean. Not a word was exchanged between us.

When I parked in front of his house, Mr. Mulcahy got out of the car and slammed the door behind him.

Only then did he turn back and look through the open window squarely into my face. After a long moment his eyes twinkled, and he said, "Young man, politically speakin' we Irish have only one weakness. We can never resist a man who says just what he thinks. Good luck to ye."

You don't have to be a liar to run for public office. It's just a lot more comfortable that way.

And this makes politics rewarding.

One Cheer for the Moral Majority

November, 1986

The September 16 issue of *Newsweek* includes an article on the increasing use of explicitly sexual appeals in advertising. Males and females, it reports, are now depicted in seductive poses and various stages of undress, as the merits of a particular product are touted. Certain feminine clothing ads are said to hint at rape, apparently to suggest that the advertised garment will drive males into a state of irresponsible passion.

One really does not need a magazine exposé in order to be acutely aware of the phenomenon described. Anyone with active glands cannot help having been conscious of this kind of exploitation for a long time. The examples featured in *Newsweek* are merely extreme illustrations of what advertisers have been up to for years. The magazine's only substantive revelation points out what are clearly homosexual appeals rather than the simple boy-meets-girl-in-the-hay.

When one dares to protest this rampant vulgarization of human sexuality he or she is likely to be told one or both of two things: no one is really influenced in any undesirable way by these ads and/or the writers of such copy are merely reflecting attitudes and values already well accepted in the American culture.

Both of these contentions are unmitigated bunk. Advertisers do not spend millions on a medium which does not significantly influence public appetites. Some of the top graduates of the best behavioral psychology departments in academe are drawn every year to Madison Avenue. And they earn their keep by concocting appeals which exploit the susceptibilities of varied constituencies.

And the contention that advertising merely reflects well-established public attitudes builds upon a wholly unrealistic doctrine of human nature. The inherent human propensity for sin is both intensified and channeled by the ethos in which men, women, and children make critical choices every day. At the very least advertising renders it easier and much more appealing to choose destructive options.

Anything which cheapens the human image strengthens the darker side of us all. Advertising which is calculated to stimulate the most intensely irresponsible appetites cannot deny its contribution to the destructive behavior that these engender.

There was a time when one might have expected Christians to mount a crusade against the denigration of human sexuality. That time, alas, is no more. Avant-garde theologians, both pastoral and academic, have in recent decades been so busy proclaiming and personally exemplifying the demise of traditional morality that mainline churches have little ground to stand on in attacking the worst abuses of the media.

During a panel discussion of this problem, one of the participants said, "Mr. Muehl seems to think that sex is dangerous." He sure does! And if right-wing religious groups, which feed on moral confusion, become potent forces in American politics, they will owe a lot to the commercial exploiters of sex and their religious apologists.

But the merchandisers of George Bush made the rest of these guys look like amateurs!

148

An Autobiographical Reflection

I was born in the bay window of my family's home on the East Side of Detroit, Michigan, in 1919. And I have been in the public eye ever since. (People only went to hospitals to die in those days.) My father was one of four children, my mother the youngest of three girls. Dad was one of Henry Ford's first dozen employees, and the family made several moves as he climbed the ladder of corporate success in the automotive industry. But not before I had acquired a brother, John, four years after my own birth.

The elementary school in Chicago, our first upward step, was something like an army camp. We marked time and marched in closed ranks from classroom to classroom, commanded by teachers who sometimes fainted in class because the depression had cut off their paychecks and their rations!

From Chicago we moved to Louisville, Kentucky, (pronounced Loyvul, not Looaville,) or a suburb called Audubon Park, where all the streets are named for birds. We lived on the corner of Thrush Road and Cardinal Drive! My school district was rural, so I attended a school as opposite to that in Chicago as one can imagine. The teachers loved us, even while they strapped us for misbehavior. And we loved them. I never felt the strap, because all Mrs. Singleton had to do when I acted up was put her hands on her hips, face me with a gimlet-eyed look and say, "You don't do things like that, Son, because you're a prince. And princes don't behave that way!"

When the depression caused the shutdown of the Ford branch that my Dad managed we moved back to Michigan, to a place called Grosse Pointe, where everybody was richer than we were. I knew that Franklin D. Roosevelt would be reelected in 1936, notwithstanding a *Literary Digest* poll to the contrary, because in a student mock election — held within a community that was a true bastion of conservative Republicanism — he got over forty-five percent of the vote.

During those high school years my Mother died very suddenly, and my Grandfather, Billy Muehl, a retired Cadillac Company employee, moved in with us. He and I did the household chores, while he reminisced about his days as a saloonkeeper and quondam beer truck driver. (A broken left arm that had been badly set made it very difficult for him to manage the team of four Percherons.)

It was during this period that I began attending a youth group at Grosse Pointe Chapel where the rector was the most intellectual human being I had met to that date, and the curate was a Socialist, not an uncommon thing among curates in an era when war veterans were selling apples on the street in order to live. When I found that the bishop, whose diocese included most of the richest families in the midwest, was a strong supporter of the Democratic Party, I decided to believe in God and have done so ever since, even during the Reagan years.

Entering the University of Michigan in 1937, I met a lot of intellectual people who did *not* believe in God. But they seemed to lack a sense of humor. So I decided to go on believing in God, for a while at any rate. I debated for all four of my college years, took part in extemporaneous speech contests all over the midwest and won most of them. I was also active in campus political groups. And the contacts that I had with Communists made me more anti-Red than all the propaganda circulated by the Hearst newspapers and the Republican Town Committee.

A treacherous digestive system kept me out of the army, despite a couple of nightmarish trips to the induction center in Detroit, where migrant agricultural workers left a trail that made it unwise to sit after them on any of the benches provided for us! I became active in the Student Religious Association, was elected its president and when the director was put in charge of alternative service camps for conscientious objectors, I was given that job on a part-time basis, because the increasingly heated war atmosphere had students more interested in rolling bandages than in talking about God.

In the fall of 1941, I began law school, from which I graduated in 1944. During my years there I won my moot court cases, but ended up in the infirmary, because the strain was too much for my tricky gut. I supported myself as a law student by teaching speech and serving as layreader for a small Episcopal church near Ann Arbor. This latter opportunity plus the job with the Student Religious Association raised the first vocational doubts I had experienced since the day in seventh grade I shocked Mrs. Singleton by telling her I wanted to be a lawyer. ("You're much too fine for that, Son!")

Then I met Ruth Daniels, a junior transfer from Wellesley College, and decided that there was more to life than winning court cases and going to the hospital afterward. So when the head of the Speech Department, an active Presbyterian layman, offered to recommend me for a post at the Yale Divinity School, I jumped at the chance. I passed the bar examinations just to prove that I could do it and moved to New Haven in September of 1944 and began a work that I have loved ever since.

Ruth and I were married that December and in due time became the proud parents of two sons, Timothy and Jonathan. We spend our summers in New Hampshire where Ruth climbs mountains, and I manufacture fabulous excuses not to go along. (Did I mention that I loathe physical exertion of any kind?) In preparation for my retirement we bought a small house in the ghost town of Bisbee, Arizona, which Ruth discovered while researching one of her articles for *Arizona Highways*. There are lots of mountains in Arizona, but there are rattlesnakes, too. So prudence will keep me from climbing them, unfortunately! We shall be spending winters in the West, summers in New Hampshire and fall and spring in our condo in Hamden, Connecticut. It will be a tough life. But, hey, nobody ever promised me a rose garden! I just stumbled into one by accident.

Summer 1989